CREATIVE CRAFTS FOR TODAY

CREATIVE CRAFTS FOR TODAY

A source book of materials and activities,
with illustrations by the author

John Portchmouth

A Studio Book
THE VIKING PRESS
New York

To my family

© John Portchmouth 1969
Second Printing May 1970
Published in 1970 by the Viking Press, Inc.
625 Madison Avenue, New York, N.Y. 10022
Library of Congress catalog card number 75-86968
First published in Great Britain by Studio Vista Ltd
Blue Star House, Highgate Hill, London, N.19
Printed Offset Litho and bound in Great Britain by
Cox & Wyman Ltd, London, Fakenham and Reading
Designed by Gillian Greenwood
SBN 670-24648-4

CONTENTS

ACKNOWLEDGEMENTS
The author acknowledges his debt to the many children, students, teachers and colleagues whose creative discoveries have helped to make this book, and to his daughter Louise for her help in checking the manuscript.

Thanks are due to the following photographers for the use of their work; Ronald P. Meyer, Front cover, and pages 13, 14, 17, 30, 33, 45, 46–49, 51, 54, 60, 67, 80, 81, 90, 95, 101, 112–114, 120, 125, 126, 138, 139, 144, 146, 148; Christopher Nelson pages 2, 15, 41, 46, 50, 52, 60, 64, 72, 73, 83, 89, 105, 113, 116, 122, 123, 126, 127, 132, 134, 136, 144; Reto Rossetti page 141.

Also to Edward Battersea, pages 113, 116, 122, Edwin G. Burton pages 60, 144 and Peter Garwood, page 135, for permission to use the works illustrated.

INTRODUCTION

When we were very young, finding ourselves on a beach was like finding we had hands. Suddenly the world was made of something we could take hold of and shape.

I don't remember how it started. There was me, and sand, and somehow there was a wooden spade: and then there were castles! I don't even remember asking how to do it; the need was big enough, and the way was there. Or maybe I'm not remembering exactly; perhaps I only found what someone had provided . . . someone who had anticipated the need.

Later on, there were things other than sand: the world was filling with more and more materials; but there were no longer the quick results, the sudden castles, that had materialised out of sand! Clay seemed to remain clay; bark obstinately stayed as bark; the old bike frame in the back yard rusted till it was taken away. Perhaps I should have progressed from castle-making to making something of these fresh experiences; but there was not the 'spade', magically there to shape them with. Maybe I did not look far enough. Sometimes, it is true, sharpening a crayon led to whittling an arrow or a peg for the garden tent; it should have been easy to go on from there and carve a man from a small branch that was nearly a man already; but it did not happen. And all the time the great world of materials was opening up or waiting to be discovered.

It helps if someone, no matter how lightly, puts in our way the means of making use of what we find . . . shows us, even, certain tools . . . talks about fitting things together . . . offers help to meet the weight and hardness and the habits of materials. With the right start we can go on.

Somewhere between the material and ourselves (about halfway between) there is an area where we come together and make a new definition—from both sides an urging and a giving way that leaves each its true character, while taking on a dimension drawn from contact with the other. It is the meeting place of the child and the sand.

This book is about the 'spade'. And about other tools, not quite as simple, that need explaining more. It is about the different processes that can help explore materials and offer means of expression through them. Information is given to support each process, but the imaginative decisions and discoveries are left to the student once he begins working. It starts wheels turning. No more.

Everyone, and children especially, I believe need to be able to create with the real everyday things they can hold, and that invite or challenge their inventiveness. It is an age of direct three-dimensional experience and expression, and the child who might reject the discipline of authority will for this reason accept the discipline of a material he can see *doing* and *becoming* something in his hands–and that carries a responsibility to him personally. The child like the adult wants the real materials of the real world to work with.

USING THIS BOOK

Under each material listed alphabetically in the main text that follows, the activities that the material lends itself to are shown.

The tools you will need for each activity are listed in the righthand column, together with a selection of other materials you may also need.

Alternative or optional materials and tools are in brackets.

On p.149 are descriptions and drawings of the tools and materials referred to.

On p.163 the Main Processes are described in full detail to save repetition in the text. For example, many materials lend themselves to mosaic work. Since the basic process is the same whether you use china pieces, glass or small stones, it is fully described under the section headed 'Mosaics and Reliefs'.

Use any other suitable materials with the main one whenever they extend the expressiveness of what you are doing. For example, if you are making a relief of tin cans, you may also find you need other shapes of metal, metal gauze, chicken wire, iron filings – or even contrasting materials like wood, glass or sand. It will help, of course, if you can build up a collection of such materials to dip into: they are often a source of further ideas in themselves. Keep in mind the value of having a wide range of materials (including those not listed) for use at any time.

ACTIVITIES IN ALPHABETICAL ORDER

ASBESTOS

You can get asbestos in the form of flat or corrugated sheeting and pieces—often as scrap from builders' or lumber yards when it has been broken. There is also a soft kind of asbestos made under different trade names (U.K. Asbestolux) which cuts and drills very easily. Use either kind, together with any other (related) materials you need.

(Roofing felt, roofing or flooring tile, insulation board, formica, slate, shingle)

1 Asbestos relief

Cut or break asbestos into different shapes, and assemble them to make a contrast of flat or corrugated surfaces.
Glue them, or drill and secure with screws.
(i) Make a simple panel relief (p. 167).
(ii) Make a plaster skimmed panel relief (p. 170).

Hand saw (hacksaw), hammer

2 Asbestos construction

Cut or break asbestos into different shapes, and assemble them as a standing or projecting form, using wood battens or strips or blocks behind them for support.

Hand saw (hacksaw), hammer
Wood battens or strips, blocks, tools for shaping and fixing these

Glue the pieces to the wood, or drill and screw them to it.

Adhesive, spreader or Metal drill, screws, awl, screwdriver

3 Asbestos—other uses

a As a surface to paint on. Irregular shaped pieces can suggest a subject by their outlines.

b As a palette on which to mix colours.

c As a modelling board.

d As a board on which to do certain plaster work.

BALLOONS

Use the shape and size of balloon that seems best.

1 Papier mâché balloon modelling

Blow up a balloon and tie it tight.
Cover it with papier mâché in layers (p. 172).

You may like to finish off with a final layer of coloured tissues or other paper.
Hang it up to dry.
When the paper has dried hard, prick the balloon. Pull it out of the small hole round the neck, and paste the hole over with paper.
You can now cut away parts from the finished shape to create light and shadow interest, and add any further decoration in the way of coloured papers, texturing materials or paint. This should, of course, relate to any shapes you have cut out.
NB *You can make the form stronger by including a layer of butter muslin strips or cheesecloth at some stage.*

(Coloured tissue, white tissue, other coloured or textured paper)

Craft knife
Paint, texturing material with adhesive

Butter muslin or cheese-cloth, scissors

2 Plaster cast 'cave' form

Use an open-ended cardboard box.
Blow up a balloon to a size that will fit into the box with 1″ or so to spare all round.
Sew two threads low down across the box to support the balloon, so that part of it will show out of the box.
Stand the balloon on the threads and sew two more threads higher up across the box the other way to hold the balloon steady.
Mix plaster (p. 172). It should be quick setting.
Pour it around the balloon.
When the plaster has set, prick the balloon.
Leave the surfaces of the 'cave' block white, with the natural contrast of light and shadow they produce, or colour them (p. 173). You can pour a thin mixture of colour into the 'cave', swill it round, and pour it out again.
You may like to make a number of these blocks and build them into a multiple construction. Join them by drilling corresponding holes in thick parts of the plaster and inserting short dowels.

Cardboard box

Thread, needle

Jug

Bowl

Drill, dowelling, saw

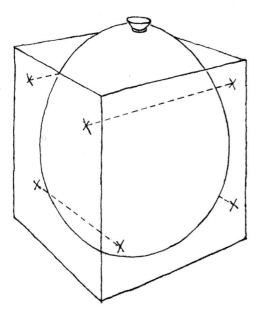

Supported balloon

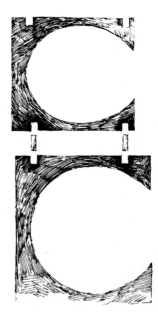

Joining the blocks

BARK

There are countless kinds of bark to be discovered in the countryside—on felled and fallen trees, in coppices, brush patches and ditches and on the floor of woods. They are all different in colour, pattern and texture. Choose the kind that is right for the job you are doing.

1 Bark study

Make a study of the colour, pattern and texture in a piece of bark, using any suitable material or process.

Materials, tools as needed

2 Bark mosaic

Break up different kinds of bark into small, fairly regular pieces. Trim them with a knife if needed. Use their contrasting surfaces:
(i) Make a simple panel mosaic (p. 167).
(ii) Make a plaster skimmed panel mosaic (p. 170).

Craft knife

3 Bark relief

Select pieces of bark for their shape, colour and texture interest. Break or trim them further if needed. The shapes should lie fairly flat.
Fit them together into a design.
(i) Make a simple panel relief (p. 167).
Glue the pieces of bark to the panel one at a time, glueing along the under-edges where they touch the panel. You may need to rub the underside of the bark on sandpaper to make it flat.
If you use a wood panel, you can fix the bark on with fine screws (drill first), panel pins or finishing nails (hammer carefully).
(ii) Make a plaster skimmed panel relief (p. 170).

Craft knife

Sandpaper

4 Bark inlay

Select pieces of bark with deeply ridged texture.
Fit them together and fix them to a board or wood panel with glue, fine screws (drill first) or panel pins (hammer carefully).

Board (wood), saw
Adhesive, spreader
or Wood drill, (awl), screws, screwdriver or Panel pins, hammer

Mix delayed setting plaster (p. 173) or cellulose filler (with powder or emulsion paint if you want it coloured) and fill in between the ridges using a kitchen knife. Fill in between the separate pieces too. Leave the tops of the ridges to stand in contrasting relief.

Plaster and size, (cellulose filler), bowl, kitchen knife, powder paint, (emulsion paint)

5 Bark carving or construction

a Find a piece of bark that resembles or suggests a form of some kind.
Carve it just enough to bring out the form.

Bark construction

Craft knife (small saw)

b Select pieces of bark that you can shape and put together to make a new form. The shape and texture of the bark may suggest something.
Either:
Fix the pieces to each other with glue or wire.

Craft knife (small saw)

Adhesive, spreader
or
Wood drill, (awl), wire, pliers

Or fix them to a light framework of battens or wood-strips with glue, wire or screws. If you wire or fasten them with screws, pierce the bark first with a drill or awl.
Both **a** and **b** can stand, hang or project.

Battens, or woodstrips, saw, panel pins, (finishing nails), hammer

Adhesive or wire as above
or
Wood drill, (awl), screws, screwdriver

6 Bark rubbing

Use a thin, strong paper.

Detail paper, (typing paper, duplicating paper)

You need to keep the paper still, but also leave a little slack to 'ride' the deeper ridges of the bark without tearing. Hold it in position on the tree or on a loose piece of bark, or fix it with pins, sellotape (U.K.) or Scotch tape (U.S.).

Dressmakers' pins (thumb tacks), sellotape (U.K.) or Scotch tape (U.S.)

Work gently but firmly to make a rubbing (p. 179).

Bark relief

BEADS

Collect an assortment of beads of different size, shape, colour and material.

1 Bead mosaic

Set out your different kinds of beads into separate piles or boxes. Arrange a design on a piece of rough fabric so that the beads will not roll. Or work directly without any pre-arrangement.

Rough fabric, e.g. felt

(i) Make a simple panel mosaic (p. 167).
(ii) Make a plaster bed mosaic (p. 168).

2 Bead appliqué

Stretch a piece of fabric across a frame by staples or by long stitches at the back, pulling it taut.

Fabric, frame, staple gun (thread, needle)

Sew different beads to it to make a design.
Use any other materials with them that you feel help the design.

Thread, needle

(Buttons, sequins, lace, braid, tape, fabric pieces)

3 Bead pendent form

Depending on the shape, you want, use rigid or flexible wire, or thread. Thread beads onto the wire or the thread to make the main shape you want. Add further 'ropes' of beads as needed to develop it, and tie them in. Join them to each other by short link wires or threads. The form can be flat or three-dimensional.
You will find it easier to work on the pendant if you hang it from a convenient point once you have the main part started.

Rigid or flexible wire, pliers,
or
Thread, scissors, needle

Wired bead shape

BONES

Use any suitable animal or bird bones:
Flattish bones like shoulder blade, breast bone, pelvis, rib and other rounder small bones.
Clean all bones thoroughly of course by boiling if necessary, though if you have time, hang them by string in the garden and the birds will do it! Or bury them for some weeks.

1 Bone study

Make a study of the shape, texture and articulation of bones, using any suitable material or process.

Materials, tools as needed

2 Bone relief

Select bones that fit together side by side in some way to make a fairly continuous surface.
(i) Make a simple panel relief (p. 167).
(ii) Make a plaster skimmed panel relief (p. 170).
Let the plaster or emulsion paint in this blend with and bond the bones.

3 Bone construction

Select suitable bones that you can combine and assemble to make a standing, hanging or projecting form. The shapes of the bones themselves may suggest an idea for this.
Fix them together by glueing them or by drilling and wiring them either to each other or to a wood support.

Adhesive, spreader
or
Metal drill, wire, pliers
Wood, saw, nails, hammer

You may find it useful to have some cellulose filler or a mixture of plaster and emulsion paint handy for filling in and bonding.

Cellulose filler (plaster and emulsion paint)

BOTTLE CAPS

1 Bottle cap mosaic

You will want an assortment of coloured caps. Some are already coloured; you can colour others with any paint. Make sure the paint is dry before you use them.
(i) Make a simple panel mosaic (p. 167).
(ii) Make a plaster bed mosaic (p. 168).
You can make some caps squarer with pliers if needed.
You will probably want to do so.

Paint

Pliers

2 Milk top mosaic

Clean the milk tops thoroughly. Press them out flat.
Colour some of them with waterproof ink (mix with a
drop or two of detergent) or transparent oil paint.
Opaque colour would lose the value of the bright metal
foil.
Let them dry.
Trim them square with scissors. Cut them into smaller
squares, not all the same size necessarily.
Make a simple panel mosaic (p. 167).

Waterproof ink, liquid
detergent
or
Transparent oil paint, see
p. 132
Scissors

3 Milk top collage

Remove the tops from bottles by pressing down with
the thumb: don't just lift off.
Clean the tops thoroughly. Lay one on the table and
press down on it with the ball of the thumb just once.
Natural creases will form in the metal foil.
With a fibre tip pen (or similar tip) work in between
them, flattening the small areas enclosed right up into
the creases, making them stand as sharp ridges. The
flat areas will take a little of the colour if you have used
a pen. You can add further colour, see above, 2.
Repeat this with the other milk tops.
Trim some of the edges a little so that the tops fit more
or less together side by side.
Make a collage (p. 165).

Fibre tip pen or similar

Colours, see above, 2

Scissors

4 Bottle cap 'cameo'

Select an attractive small
object that will fit easily into
a metal bottle cap.

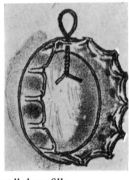

Pebble (piece of thick
glass—clear, coloured,
weathered, mirror—broken
china, metal object—
machine part, shell,
large bead, gem, button)

Cap wired for pendant

Plaster (cellulose filler)

Mix some plaster (p. 172) or cellulose filler.
Fill the bottle cap with it to just below the rim, and set
the object in it, wiping away any overspill.
Colour the plaster (p. 173) or filler if needed.
(If you think you will want to use the cameo as a pendant, make a small hole in the edge with an awl before
you start, and twist a loop of fine wire through it as an
'eye' for any thread or chain.)
You could also make a number of these cameos and
make a plaster bed mosaic (p. 168).

Awl, hammer, wire, pliers

5 Bottle cap impressions

Prepare a clay slab for making impressions (p. 163).

Press one or more bottle caps, either way up, into the clay to make a pattern of impressions. Remove after each impression, of course. Let the impressions touch or overlap as needed.
(i) Biscuit/glaze fire the slab (p. 163) or
(ii) Make a plaster cast (p. 174).
Colour the cast if needed (p. 174).

6 Bottle cap print

Press a bottle cap, either way up, into a foam plastic pad of paint or ink, and make a pattern of the prints (p. 175).
You will get a clearer print if you have a few sheets of newspaper under the printing paper.

Foam plastic

Newspaper

BOTTLES

Bottles (especially the coloured ones) are mainly useful as broken glass for mosaic and stained glass work (see Glass, p. 61).
Other uses:
a For storing made-up ink, dye, paint.

b As a support for a puppet head or similar model while you are making it.

c As a stand for a glove puppet in a display.

d As a 'rolling pin' for making a clay slab (straight-sided bottle only).

BRICKS

1 Brick carving

Use the softer building brick (it is lighter in colour). A builder will tell you of local sources of supply. The normal brick is too hard to carve: it splits easily.
Stand the brick on sacking or in a sand box. Work directly, or from a prepared sketch, and carve it with any cutting edge you find suitable. A good penknife will often do. Keep the shape fairly simple.

Sacking (sand box)

Penknife (stone chisel gouge, hacksaw blade, large nail, stone rasp, riffler)

2 Brick construction

It is not too much to say that a brick construction can still be original. Use whole or parts of bricks (trim off with a trowel edge). Build them up with a 1:3 cement/

Trowel

sand mix, varying the arrangement, the angle, the projection, the colour of the bricks to make a 'wall' or 'walkround' form in an open space outdoors.

Cement, sand, shovel, board

Use the cement to fill spaces and to do any extra surface modelling needed, but only add it sparingly, especially to upright surfaces, and allow a day or so for it to set off before adding more–otherwise it may fall away.

You may find it interesting to include other related materials that the cement can bond; though again allow enough time for setting off.

(Building block, stone, slate, tile, metal)

3 Bricks–other uses

The bricks should be clean and dry.

a To weight collage and relief materials while they are sticking.

b As a platform for drying out home-dug clay. Spread brown wrapping paper over it first.

c As supports for low shelving. Just lay them on top of each other: the weight of the shelves and things on them should keep them steady.

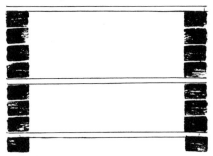

BUILDING BLOCKS

The original coarse building block (known as breeze block), used mainly for inner walls of buildings, has been joined by a more refined one with a smoother texture (cinder or Celcon block). This is particularly easy to carve, though its pale grey colour lacks character. (It can gain character from the way it is carved). It can be recognised on most building sites, and the builder would be able to tell you of local sources of supply.

1 Building block carving

You can use a good penknife, stone chisel, gouge, and other home-made tools to carve the block–and get considerable detail despite its somewhat brittle nature.

a Carving in the round:

Set up the block on a bench. A piece of sacking or a sand box will cushion it and help to keep it steady, as well as restricting the dust.

Carve directly into the block, using any suitable tool, discovering forms and surface texture as you go along.

Sacking (sand box)
Penknife (stone chisel, gouge, hacksaw blade, large nail, stone rasp, Bouchard hammer, mallet, plaster rasp, riffler)

If you prefer, make a sketch on paper of the shape you want to carve. Refer to it from time to time as you work. Start by marking the highest points on the block with chalk. Carve away from these points down to the deeper levels. Turn the block as you need to. You can finish off with a stone or plaster rasp if you want a smooth surface.

Smaller pieces broken off a block are sometimes quite suitable for carving, and you can do this comfortably in the hands.

Drawing medium, paper

Chalk

b Carving in relief:

Lay the block flat on a bench with some sacking underneath to cushion it and save the dust.

Carve directly into the block (tools, see above) discovering relief forms and textures as you go.

You may prefer to make a sketch on paper of the design you want to carve. Refer to it from time to time as you work. Start by marking the highest points on the block with chalk. Carve away from these points down to the deeper levels (tools, see above).

Sacking

Tools, see above, a

Drawing medium, paper

Chalk
Tools, see above, a

2 Building block dust relief

Use the dust from the cement breeze block or Celcon or cinder block (saved from a previous carving perhaps). Make a glued relief (p. 166).
Use any other similar material for contrast if needed.

(Sand, stone dust, slate dust, brick dust, coal dust, coke dust, clinker dust, birdcage grit, glitter, metal filings, rust dust, sawdust, chalk dust)

3 Building block dust–rubbing/print

Make a clearly defined glued relief, see above, 2.
Keep the dust fairly fine or it may cut into the paper during the rubbing or printing.
(i)   Make a rubbing (p. 179).
(ii) Make a roll-through print (p. 176).
(iii) Ink and make a print (p. 175).

See above, 2

BUTTONS

1 Button mosaic

Use whole or broken buttons of any kind (bone, plastic, metal, wood). You may want to paint some of them. Use any suitable paint. Let it dry.
(i) Make a simple panel mosaic (p. 167).
(ii) Make a plaster skimmed panel mosaic (p. 170).

Paint

2 Button impression

Prepare a clay slab for making impressions (p. 163).
Use both sides of different buttons. Press them into the
clay and lift them out, leaving an impressed design.
(i) Biscuit/glaze fire the slab (p. 163) or
(ii) Make a plaster cast (p. 174).
Colour the cast if needed (p. 174).

3 Button print

Press a small ball of plasticine onto the back of a button.   Plasticine
Use this to hold it by. You can press the plasticine
through any holes in the button so that they print as
part of its shape.
Make a pattern of prints (p. 175).

CANDLES

1 Candle wax resist

a Draw with a sharpened candle end on paper, pres-   Drawing paper, craft knife
sing fairly firmly.   (penknife)
Mix some watercolour or thinned powder paint, a   Water colour (powder
different colour from the paper, and paint evenly over   paint)
the whole paper. The parts drawn with the candle will
resist the paint.

NB *Be careful of fire risk in the following. Keep wax away
from the heat source.*
b Melt a candle with a little white spirit in a double   Double saucepan (tin can,
saucepan or a tin can in a pan of water. Keep the wax   pan), white spirit
warm while you are using it.
Dip a brush in the wax and draw direct onto a sheet of   Drawing paper, brush
paper.
Colour wash the paper.   Water colour (powder
When the paint is dry, iron out the wax through a sheet   paint)
of brown paper (have some old newspapers under the   Flat iron, brown paper,
drawing). The design will become clear against the   newspaper
colour.

c Melt a candle as above, **b**.   See above, b
Stretch and pin a piece of fabric to a board. (News-   Fabric, thumb tacks,
paper padding under the fabric will prevent wax spoil-   board, newspaper
ing the board).
Dip a brush in the wax and draw direct onto the fabric.   Brush
Repeat the design on the back.
Mix some cold water dye. Immerse and leave the fabric   Cold water dye, bowl
in it for the required period.
Stretch the fabric out on the board again, and iron out
the wax through a sheet of brown paper. The design   Flat iron, brown paper,
will become clear against the dye colour.   newspaper

2 Candle 'free fall' modelling

Wire armature

NB *Be careful of fire risk and melted wax.*
a Light a candle. Hold it at an angle over a board and let its drips fall on each other to make a rising shape.

b Twist some wire into a small shape as a support (or armature) for the wax.
Staple it to a wood block if needed.
Light the candle. Hold it at an angle over the wire model and let its drips build up the shapes. Overloaded and unsupported wax may break off.
You can smooth or model the wax further with a warm knife if needed.

Wire, pliers

Staples, hammer (staple gun), wood block

Kitchen knife (craft knife)

3 Candle carving

Use any candle of standard (or larger) size.
Carve it with a craft knife or penknife. As your hands warm the candle it will become a little softer to carve.
Or you can warm the candle specially beforehand.
Leave the wick as part of the carving, or snip it off.
A warmed knife will give a different carved surface.
Support the finished carving if appropriate, e.g. on a warmed nail through a wood block.

Craft knife (penknife)

Nail, hammer, wood block

4 Candle rubbing

Use a candle to make a rubbing of a surface (p. 179).

CANDY (SWEET) WRAPPERS

Use colourful confectionery wrappings of all kinds as well as the smaller individual wrappers.

1 Wrapper collage

Sort out wrappers of different colour, pattern and transparency. Smooth them out, pressing any obstinate ones in a heavy book–unless, of course, you want to use them crumpled.

Book

Make a collage (p. 165), pasting the wrappers to get the most from their particular qualities.

2 Wrapper mosaic

Cut up the wrappers into smaller squarish shapes.
Use a good selection of bright and transparent colours and different metallic foils.

Scissors

Make a simple panel mosaic (p. 167).

3 Wrapper windows

Cut two pieces of cardboard the same shape.
Cut an arrangement of small windows or openings to correspond in each of them.

Cardboard, craft knife (scissors)

Using transparent wrappers singly or overlaid, paste them across the windows of one card. Then stick the other card to it, making a sandwich of the wrappers.
Set it up against the light.

Adhesive, spreader

4 Wrapper slide

Make slides for use with a projector (say $2'' \times 2''$).
Use only transparent coloured papers.

Projector (screen)

a Cut two cardboard squares, $2'' \times 2''$. Cut a corresponding window in each.

Cardboard, craft knife (scissors)

Glue the wrappers in an overlapping arrangement so that you have different thicknesses in different parts of the window. Sandwich and glue them between the cardboard squares. Project onto a screen or light wall.

Adhesive, spreader

b Cut two squares of thin glass, $2'' \times 2''$.
Glue the wrappers as above, **a**, and sandwich them between the glass squares. Edge the squares with Scotch tape (U.S.) Sellotape (U.K.). Project onto a screen or light wall.

Thin glass, glass cutter
See above, a
Sellotape or Scotch tape, scissors

CANE (REED)

You can use any thickness of cane or reed, and combine different thicknesses in the same job.
Soak the canes or reeds first in a sink to make them supple, and damp them from time to time while you are using them if they dry off.

1 Cane or reed relief

Cut a suitable board or wood panel.
Cut off a length of cane or reed and bend it into a flat

Saw
Chipboard (blockboard,

shape. Fix it to the panel with panel pins or finishing nails. Use as few pins as possible.

Continue cutting and adding cane or reed in the same way to complete your design. Cut ends neatly at an angle where they meet others.

This may be a satisfactory 'line' design in itself, or you may wish to colour or texture some of the enclosed areas with other materials.

wood)
Craft knife (side cutters, secateurs or shears)
Panel pins or finishing nails, hammer
Paint (ink, wood stain)
or
Sand (sawdust, bark, bast or fibrous bark, woody plant, dried plant, seed) with adhesive

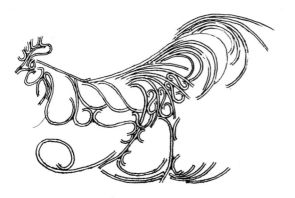

Cane relief

2 Cane or reed modelling

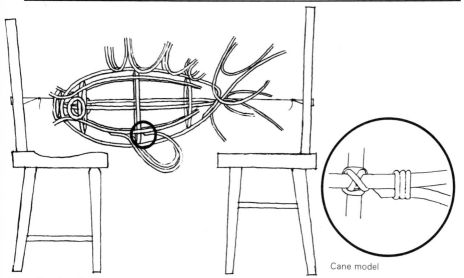

Cane model

a Bend and tie a length of cane or reed into a flat shape, cutting it as needed. Suspend it by tying it between two chair tops or other available points so that you can work all round it.

Cut, bend and tie further lengths of cane or reed into this, developing it outwards to make an open-work form. Trim off any unwanted ends.

This may be a satisfactory 'line model' in space.

b Make a model as above, **a**.

Cut and glue shapes of other materials to fill some or all of the planes created by the canes. Trim each piece of material off along the cane as you finish.

String (thread, twine, raffia)
Craft knife (side-cutters, secateurs or shears)

Strong tissue (imitation Japanese rice paper, cellophane, acetate sheeting, organdie, butter muslin or cheesecloth, net)
Scissors
Adhesive, spreader

c Make a model as above, **a**.
Select some lengths of thread.
Run a thin line of glue along the edges of canes or reeds forming a plane. Working from one end to the other, wind the thread across and round the canes (not too tight: it will distort the cane). Glue only as much as you can wind before the glue dries. Join new lengths neatly *on* the cane. Wind the thread close or spaced depending on the effect you want. Interesting crossing of planes will develop, and could be made use of.

Button thread (parcel string, gardening twine, gift string, embroidery cotton)
Adhesive, spreader
Scissors

d Make a basic framework of wood as close as possible to the cane or reed shape you have in mind. Joint or screw together the parts securely. Glue meeting surfaces for extra strength.
Cut and bend canes or reeds to go across or round the framework. Fix them with panel pins or finishing nails, supporting the framework from behind with a heavy hammer or similar weighty object at the point you are nailing. Trim off ends after nailing if possible to avoid splitting. Lay the canes or reeds close or spaced, depending on the effect you want.

Wood, saw, chisel, mallet, screws, awl, wood drill, screwdriver, Adhesive, spreader
Craft knife (side-cutters, secateurs), panel pins or finishing nails, hammer, heavy hammer (similar weighty object)

CARDBOARD

Use any of the kinds of cardboard listed (p. 154) including any off-cuts from work with other crafts.

1 Cardboard collage

Cut different shapes of cardboard, using any contrast of colour, thickness or texture.
Make a collage (p. 165) with the card flat in one or more layers.

Craft knife (scissors)

2 Cardboard mosaic

Cut up different kinds of cardboard into small, squarish shapes.
Using any contrast of size, colour, thickness or texture, make a simple panel mosaic (p. 167).

Craft knife (scissors)

3 Cardboard relief

Cut different shapes and kinds of cardboard.
Use them flat (any number of layers); on edge; scored and bent into various shapes; or damped and shaped into curves (hold the shape in position by any suitable means until it is dry: it will then keep its shape).

Craft knife (scissors)
Sponge
String (elastic band, paper clip, foldback clip, bulldog clip, clothes' peg or clothes' pin, thumb tacks in board)

Make a simple panel relief (p. 167) sticking the pieces on one at a time and making sure each is fixed well before going on to the next.
Introduce colour or texture at any stage if needed, but if you make the cardboard too wet, it will buckle.

Paint, texturing material with adhesive

4 Cardboard engraving

Use a thicker cardboard like strawboard.
Draw and engrave a design on it with a pointed or gouge shaped instrument.

Divider (compass, awl, large nail, bodkin, linoleum cutter)

Paint the cardboard with ink or powder paint. Wipe it with a flat foam plastic sponge to remove some of the surface colour. The denser colour will remain in the etched lines as contrast.
You can heighten this contrast by waxing the flat cardboard with a candle before painting to resist the colour.

Ink (powder paint)
Foam plastic sponge

Candle

5 Cardboard construction

Cut cardboard to different shapes to assemble as a standing, hanging or projecting form. Use the cardboard in flat planes, or shape it by scoring and bending, or by damping and curving it as needed. If you damp and curve it, hold the shape in position by any suitable means until it is dry. It will then keep its shape.

Craft knife (scissors)

Sponge
String (elastic band, paper clip, foldback clip, bulldog clip, clothes' peg or clothes' pin, thumb tacks in board)
Adhesive, spreader

You can glue some of these pieces together by their own edges or sides. To glue others: score and bend them over to make flaps; cut a separate angle strip to put behind to which to glue them; or cut small blocks or strips of wood (balsa will do) to which to glue them. Make sure each part adheres well before joining others. You can colour or texture the construction before, during or after assembly if needed, but if you make the cardboard too wet, it will buckle.

Balsa or other suitable wood, saw
Powder paint (emulsion paint), texturing material with adhesive

6 Cardboard rubbing/print

Make a *flat* cardboard collage (1) or mosaic (2)
(i)   Make a rubbing (p. 179).
(ii) Make a roll-through print (p. 176).
(iii) Ink and make a print (p. 175).

See above (1) or (2)

7 Cardboard plaster cast

Make a cardboard collage (1) or mosaic (2)
Make a plaster cast of it (p. 174).
Either:
(i)   Colour the cast (p. 174).
(ii) Make a rubbing of it (p. 179).
(iii) Ink and make a print (p. 175).

See above (1) or (2)

8 Cardboard – other uses

a As a painting surface. Prime it first with size, glue or emulsion paint if you are using oil paint.

Size (glue, emulsion paint), pan, broad brush

b As a mount for another light collage, mosaic or relief.

c Strips of cardboard as painting tools.

CARDBOARD BOXES

Use any shape or size of box.

Box sculpture

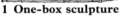

1 One-box sculpture

a Make cuts down the corners and sides of a box. Bend the sides inwards and outwards either in curves, or sharply along scored lines. Cut further into the sides, and bend as needed. Use any combination of cuts, curves and bends to get the shape you want. Glue meeting edges one at a time.

Craft knife (scissors)

Adhesive, spreader

You can paint the resulting planes for colour effect or contrast of lighting, but if you make the cardboard too wet it will buckle.

Powder paint (emulsion paint)

The visual effect will be different if you fix the box so that it projects from a vertical surface.

You may choose to make a number of one-box sculptures and group them to stand or project as an assembled form. Decide on the overall colour effect and paint them before assembly as far as possible.

b Make cuts into a box, as above, **a**, but remove some parts completely. Each part you remove, glue back onto the remaining form in a different place. Try various placings before fixing.

See above, a

2 Grouped-box sculpture

Trim and cut boxes to different shapes and build them to make a standing or projecting form or a relief. Glue the units one at a time. Wait till each has set before going on to the next, or the structure may come apart behind you. A few touches of glue should be enough except along joined edges facing outwards: glue these tight all along. Foldback or bulldog clips or clothes' pins will hold these while they are setting.

Craft knife (scissors)
Board (for a relief)
Adhesive, spreader

Foldback clips (bulldog clips, clothes' pins)

You can face the boxes either way and at various angles to each other. Make full use of the differences in depth and size to create all-round or frontal interest, depending on the effect you want. You can also set them inside each other.

Paint or cover the finished forms with different materials if needed to give greater unity or variety.

Powder paint, (emulsion paint), texturing material with adhesive

3 String-box sculpture

Cut one end out of a box.
Paint it inside and out or cover with different materials if needed.

Prick corresponding patterns of holes in opposing sides of the box.
Following whatever plan seems best, sew thread, twine or string across the inside of the box from side to side, making a regulated pattern of crossing lines. Make any joins neatly up against a hole, or secure the ends with a bead of glue.
The colour of the line is important. Consider it in relation to the colour of the box.
You could make a number of these and assemble them as grouped-box sculpture in a standing or projecting form or in a relief. The lighting inside is clearly important.

Craft knife (scissors)
Powder paint (emulsion paint), texturing material with adhesive
Needle (bodkin or piercing awl)
Thread (twine, string)

Glue

4 Cardboard box–other uses

a Cut down boxes and cartons and use the sides for painting, collage and other flat designs.

b Use shallow or cut-down boxes, or box lids as beds for mosaic and light relief work.

c Use boxes for storage for scrap and other materials.

CARDS (GREETING)

1 Greeting card mosaic

Cut up greeting cards into small squares or similar shapes. Get as much variety as possible of colour and glitter.
Mix up the pieces and assemble them into a new design.
Make a simple panel mosaic (p. 167).

Craft knife (scissors)

CARTRIDGE (HEAVY DRAWING) PAPER

1 Paper counter-change

Cut a sheet of cartridge paper and a sheet of black or coloured paper twice as large.
Cut away shapes from the cartridge paper with a craft knife.

Black or coloured paper

Craft knife

Counterchange

Place what is left of the cartridge paper over one half of the coloured paper, which will show through the cut-away parts. Paste it down.

Adhesive, spreader

Arrange the cut-away shapes themselves on the other coloured half–opposite the holes they left. Paste them down.

The white and coloured areas on one side will now correspond with the coloured and white areas opposite.

2 Paper collage

Cut or tear the cartridge paper freely into various shapes.

Craft knife (scissors)

Make a collage (p. 165).

3 Paper mosaic

Cut the cartridge paper into strips of various widths, mostly between $\frac{1}{4}''$ and $1''$.

Craft knife (scissors)

Cut the strips into squares.

Using the different sized squares to best effect, make a simple panel mosaic (p. 167).

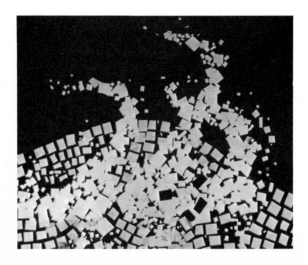

Paper mosaic

4 Paper strip relief

Cut the cartridge paper into various shaped strips. Nip these at irregular intervals so that they bend and curve. Arrange these 'undulating' strips on a piece of cardboard into a design. Space, touch or overlap them. Glue them at the points of contact.

Craft knife (scissors)

Cardboard
Adhesive, spreader

5 Paper spiral relief

Cut cartridge paper into strips of various widths.
With one hand, hold the end of a strip between the thumb and a ruler (or any straight edge). With the other hand, draw the strip smoothly down towards you. Repeating this will tighten the spiral.
Arrange an assortment of spirals (different widths and tensions) into a design on a cardboard or board panel. Space, meet or interlock them.
Touch across the underneath edges of each spiral with paste, gum or glue, and lay it in place. Hold it for a few moments to prevent it unwinding.

Craft knife (scissors)
Ruler or similar straight edge

Cardboard (board)

Adhesive, spreader

Curling paper

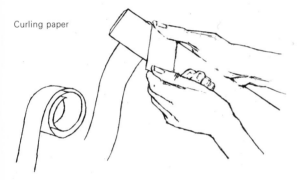

6 Paper sculpture

Cut a shape from cartridge paper.
Cut into it from different sides and score on either side with a kitchen knife or other suitable tool between the cuts. Fold the paper along the scored lines.
Develop the shape that results by further cutting, scoring and bending.
Lightly glue, or slot, any meeting edges or surfaces you need to.
Cut any further shapes of paper needed to complete the form, and fix them to it.
To make the paper curve or curl, roll it a few times round a rounded shape, or draw it smoothly downwards between your thumb and a ruler or any straight edge.
You can make endless shapes by varying and combining these processes, planning for more controlled effects with experience.

Craft knife (scissors)

Kitchen knife or similar instrument

Adhesive, spreader

Rounded object
Ruler or similar straight edge

7 Paper rubbing

From a paper counter-change (1), a flat paper collage (2), or a paper mosaic (3), make a rubbing (p. 179).

8 Paper print

Paper print

a Use glue instead of paste or gum to make a paper counter-change (1), a flat paper collage (2) or a paper mosaic (3).
(i) Make a roll-through print (p. 176).
(ii) Ink it and make a print (p. 175).

b Make a masked print (p. 175).

Crumpled paper print

c Make a crumpled paper print.
Crumple a sheet of cartridge paper with varying pressures.
Put out printing ink on an inking plate.

Inking plate, printing ink, roller

Ink a roller and roll out across the ridges of the crumpled paper.
When the ink is dry, iron out the paper under a sheet of scrap paper.

Flat iron, scrap paper

CHALK

1 Chalk carving

Chalk found along the tide line on beaches is soft to carve. Chalk from land pits is harder and more brittle. Both carve nicely.
Look for forms suggested by the natural shape of the

Chalk carving. Child

block. Turn it the best way for carving, and stand it on a piece of folded sacking to cushion it a little and to save the chalk dust (it can be used in other crafts); or bed it in a seed box filled with sand to keep it steady. You can carve small pieces in the hands, of course.

Sacking (seed box of sand)

Carve it with any suitable tool. Avoid too much hammering: it could shatter the chalk.

Craft knife (kitchen knife, pen knife, chisel, gouge, file, plaster rasp, hacksaw blade, grater, large nail, nail file, riffler)

Sand box

You can smooth any surfaces you want to with sand-paper. Clear the sandpaper of chalk by flicking it from the back with the finger.

Sandpaper

Some flat pieces of chalk may lend themselves more to a relief carving.

2 Chalk dust relief

Save any chalk dust from carving.
Use it by itself on a contrasting panel, or with other similar materials.

(Sand, stone dust, slate dust, brick dust, building block dust, coal dust, coke dust, clinker dust, bird-cage grit, glitter, metal filings, rust dust, sawdust)

Make a glued relief (p. 166).

CHICKEN WIRE

1 Chicken wire modelling

a Model a piece of chicken wire into a shape. Cut into it from the edges with side cutters or pliers as needed. Turn any ends over and twist them neatly into the mesh, or trim them off.

Side cutters (pliers)

b Cut a number of smaller pieces of chicken wire to form the sides or planes of a model. Fasten the edges neatly all along by bending the wire ends into the adjoining ones.

Side cutters (pliers)

c Use left-over scraps of chicken wire with other materials to make a model.
a, **b**, and **c** can all be designed to stand, hang or project.

Side cutters (pliers) (Wire, wire gauze, punched bars, metal scrap, wood, cardboard, board, hessian or burlap—with tools)

2 Covered chicken wire modelling

Model the chicken wire to stand, hang or project, see above, 1—but as a base for covering with another material later. Tuck in all sharp ends of wire.
Tear or cut strips of paper or fabric.

Side cutters (pliers)

Scissors
Newspaper (brown paper, wrapping paper) butter muslin, or cheesecloth (scrim or burlap, hessian or other fabric)

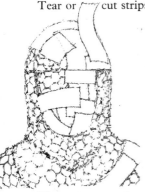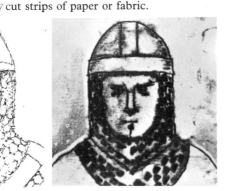

Covering chicken wire

If you are covering the model with paper, soak the paper in paste.
If you are covering it with fabric, soak the fabric in thin glue, delayed setting plaster, cellulose filler or emulsion paint, or in any mixture of these.
Lay the strips on the chicken wire, pressing them down gently until they are well stuck and the wire completely covered where you want it. You may need more layers, and you can add these straight away. You can press into the texture of the wire to give a different surface effect to your last layer, or leave the mesh exposed in parts where it helps. When the final covering is dry (next day probably) you can paint it, or add further materials to complete its surface effect.

Paste, bowl

Scotch glue, glue pot
or
Plaster with size, pan, bowl
or
Cellulose filler, bowl
or
Emulsion paint, bowl
Ink (dye, paint), texturing material with adhesive

3 Chicken wire relief

Cut and form shallow shapes from chicken wire, using scraps left over from chicken wire modelling if you have them—together with any other related materials.
(i) Make a simple panel relief (p. 167).

Side cutters (pliers)

See above, 1c

(ii) Make a plaster skimmed panel relief (p. 170).

4 Chicken wire weaving

Cut out a shape of $\frac{1}{2}''$ chicken wire.
Cut strips of any fabric (not too flimsy).
Weave the strips into the chicken wire, working from side to side, or in various directions to make a free design. To join, or start a new colour, bend the new strip with a twist or two to the one in use, securing with a stitch or a touch of glue if needed.

Side cutters (pliers)
Fabric, scissors

Thread, needle
(adhesive, spreader)

5 Chicken wire print

Cut a shape of chicken wire. Remove any sharp ends.
Lay it flat on a board.
Lay a printing paper over it (a slightly stronger kind preferably) and pin it down.
(i) Make a roll-through print (p. 176).
Move the chicken wire a little under the paper and make a second print on top of the first. By continuing to move the wire, and perhaps change the colour of the printing ink, you can make a more and more intricate design. Stop at the one you like.
(ii) Moving the wire in the same way, ink it and make a print (p. 175).

Side cutters (pliers)
Board

CHINA

1 China mosaic

Use old or unwanted china, plain or decorated: plates, saucers, flat dishes and bowls, ceramic tiles, china ornaments, other fairly flat ware.
Protect the eyes and hands where necessary.
Wrap the pieces in sacking and break them up on a board, a stone floor or path. The pieces should be fairly small and not too curved; but you can make use of all kinds of shape otherwise.
(i) Make a simple panel mosaic (p. 167).
(ii) Make a plaster bed mosaic (p. 168).
You can, of course, use other materials with the broken china if they help.

Eyeshield, leather gloves
Sacking, board, hammer

(Glass—clear, stained, mirror, dimpled, reeded, frosted, reinforced, weathered—slate, marble, flat stone, hard plastic)

2 China–other uses

a Use a plate or saucer as a mixing palette for all kinds of painting.

b Use cups and bowls for mixing paste, plaster and other things in.

c Use a jug for pouring paint, plaster and other mixtures.

CHIPPINGS

Chippings here include such things as gravel, pebble dash, small flints, marble chips (white, red and green), stone chips and coal fragments.

1 Chippings mosaic

Sort out chippings into different kinds, colours and textures, so that you have separate lots to choose from.
(i) Make a simple panel mosaic (p. 167).
(ii) Make a plaster bed mosaic (p. 168).

CHRISTMAS TREE DECORATIONS

1 Decorations mosaic

Use broken Christmas tree decorations made of glass or plastic, or other similar light-weight baubles. Break them into smaller pieces (*careful of splinters*). | Hammer, pliers, scissors
(i) Make a simple panel mosaic (p. 167).
(ii) Make a plaster skimmed panel mosaic (p. 170).

CLAY

You can use prepared clay from a dealer (see p. 154) or clay you have dug yourself, though for firing purposes you may have to mix this with a prepared clay, as by itself it would melt at higher temperatures. If you are going to try it, test fire a small piece first at lower temperatures and see how it stands up.

To prepare your own clay:

Look out for places where weather or land and river movements have brought clay to the surface, or where excavations have been carried out for new roads and buildings and for underground cables and pipes. When you have collected the clay, let it dry and then break it into small pieces. Leave it soaking in a bucket of water till it softens and you can mix it all up (stir it on and off during this time). Work it through a sieve (size 50 will do) and let it stand in a bucket until the clay has sunk and you can drain the water off. Put the clay out on a slab of plaster or on a platform of bricks covered with brown paper. After a while you can gather the clay up and wedge it to a good working consistency. Whatever clay you use, have it in good condition before you start. It should squeeze and shape easily without being sticky.

Spade (shovel), mallet, bucket

Sieve

Plaster slab (bricks, brown paper)

Clay you receive in good condition can just be kneaded: put out a fair-sized ball of clay on a bench; pressing down with the hands, work it with a rocking and rotating movement until it is uniformly even.

Other clay may need wedging.

You can wedge a small lump in your hands: twist it in two, and slap the halves together; turn them and repeat the action; go on doing this until the clay is right.

Wedge a larger lump on the bench: use wire or nylon attached to toggles (you could whittle these yourself); draw the wire through the lump; turn the halves and bang them together with different sides meeting; slice again (moisten by sprinkling with a little water if needed) and repeat the action; go on doing this until the clay is right. The help of a partner makes this much easier.

Clay in this state can now be kneaded.

When the clay is in the right condition, keep it airtight in a closed container or a plastic bag when you are not actually using it.

Keep hands moist while handling clay.

Wire (nylon), toggles

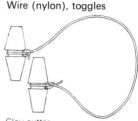

Clay cutter
Air-tight bin (plastic bag)

1 Clay modelling

Have a board handy: you may want to work on it from the start or from time to time. Shape the clay freely in the hands, adding or taking clay away to make the form. The squeezing and handling of the clay can suggest forms that might be developed. Keep the lower part fairly sturdy, as it supports the rest. Very thin shapes tend to dry out fast and crack.

You can do much of the modelling with just your hands, but you may find you need simple tools for details and different surface effects.

Small board

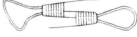

Looped-wire tool

Small shaped piece of wood, metal or hard plastic, lollypop stick, broken and shaped ruler end, nail file, loop of stout wire, broken hacksaw blade, kitchen knife, spoon, fork, boxwood spatula, wire-ended modelling tool

To prevent thick models cracking as they dry, remove some of the clay from inside them with a looped-wire tool or another that is suitable. Do this before you have got too far with any detail modelling of the surface, as this may suffer while you are hollowing. (This is especially necessary if you are going to fire the model finally. But it helps either way).

Clay model. Child

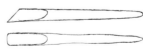

Boxwood tool

2 Clay tile

Mix a little coarse grog or sand with the clay before you start. This will help prevent the tile warping as it dries.

Grog (sand)

The tile should also be kept flat. If you make several, stack them on top of each other when they are finished if possible.

Prepare the clay as a slab for making impressions (p. 163).

Decorate it in any of these ways (or other ways you can):
Use your fingers and nails to make a surface design.

Press small objects into the clay to make a design of the impressions. Lift each one off cleanly after use.

Small machine part—cog, spring, lever, nut, bolt—screw, shell, fern . . . the list is endless of course

Engrave lines and textures in the clay with any suitable tool.

Small shaped piece of . . wood, metal or hard plastic, lollypop stick, broken and shaped ruler end, nail file, broken hacksaw blade, kitchen knife, spoon, fork, old ball-point pen . . again the list is endless

Build up a relief pattern of coils, balls, pellets and other clay pieces pressed gently into the clay. Pressing them in deeper gives a different effect. Using a different coloured clay for this gives a different effect again.

Model more boldly and freely onto the slab by adding and taking away clay, building up a deeper relief.

Tools, as above

Decorate or build up the tile with any combination of the above processes.

You can leave the finished tile as it is (though it will remain brittle in this condition), or
(i) Biscuit/glaze fire it (p. 163), or
(ii) Make a plaster cast of it (p. 174).
Colour the plaster if needed (p. 174).

3 Simple clay pots

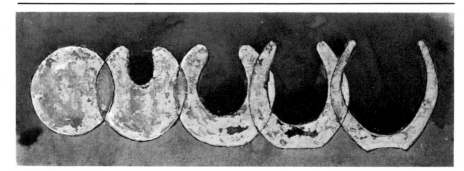

A pinch or thumb pot

Roll the clay into a ball (golf to billiard size). Hold it in the cupped hand. Push the other thumb down into the centre. Squeeze the clay gently between the thumb and fingers, rotating the clay through them. Press the thumb in deeper and go on rotating and squeezing. As you continue doing this, the pot will get bigger and the walls and base thinner. Let your hands shape the form roundly. Stop when the shape is pleasant to hold and wall thickness feels right for the size. Finish off by flattening the bottom slightly, along with any un-wanted irregularities of the sides or lip.

You can texture the pot (sometimes best done with it turned upside down). Use any suitable tool–or pat it gently to a smooth firm finish with a piece of wood.

You can join thumb pots to each other (use thick slip, and tool across the meeting edges), or model on them with more clay to make other shapes. If you enclose a space between pots by doing this, make an escape hole for the air if you want to fire them (p. 163).

A coil pot

Shape the clay into 'ropes' in the hands, or by rolling it backwards and forwards on a table, keeping your hands flat and working outwards from the centre. Press lightly and try to keep the rolls round and the same thickness all the time (about the thickness of your finger or thumb). The clay should coil round the finger without cracking.

Keep rolls under a damp cloth till you use them.

Roll another piece of clay into a ball (golf to billiard size). Flatten it with the palm of the hand on a piece of hessian or burlap to prevent it sticking to the table. Turn the clay over from time to time until it is about $\frac{1}{2}''-1''$ thick, depending on the size the pot will be. Trim it with a knife to the shape you want for the base, e.g. round, oval, square. Moisten and tool round the edge with the tip of the knife. Coil the first rope onto it, pressing gently. Nip off the end and join up smoothly. Work round the join, thumbing the base to the coil to make a good connection on one or both sides. Moisten and tool the coil and add a second one, thumbing this in the same way to the coil beneath. Continue doing this with the rest of the coils, increasing or decreasing their length to make the shape move out or in; but don't curve outwards too much or the wall will sag. Watch the profile and general shape of the pot as it rises; keep turning it to check that all is well.

Smooth the coils to each other on the inside as you go along: at each increase in height it becomes less easy to get at them.

You can leave the outside unthumbed, or thumbed, or you can work it over with a tool like a hacksaw blade, or smooth it down more thoroughly. It depends on the effect you want.

You can, of course, use the coiling process to raise models of different kinds, e.g. figures, animals.

A pinch and coil pot

Make a pinch or thumb pot and build onto it with coils. You can use this process to make models of different kinds, e.g. figures, animals.

A slab pot

Make a base as in a coil pot.

Prepare a clay slab of suitable thickness, as for making impressions (p. 163).

Cut shapes from it to make the sides of the pot.

Put thick slip round the edge of the base. Stand the wall slabs on it and press them well together. Run a coil of clay along the join and press it in to make a better connection. Join any edges of walls that meet each other as you go along in the same way.

Texture or smooth the pot as needed.

You can use this process to make other kinds of model, e.g. buildings, abstract forms.

Joined thumb pots

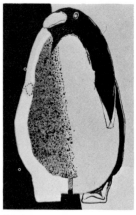

Cloth

Hessian or burlap

Knife

Hacksaw blade, or similar tool

See above

See above

Knife

Tools, see above, 2

4 Clay mosaic

Prepare a clay slab as for making impressions (p. 163). Allow it time to harden off a little: it will cut better.	
Mark out the clay into squares with the tip of a knife.	Knife
Cut it into strips one way without going right through. This keeps them together for the next step. Cut it into strips the other way, going right through this time.	Straight edge
Finish the cutting of the first strips.	
You can cut these squares into smaller ones, giving more variety of size.	
If the knife sticks at all during the cutting, put a little machine oil on it.	Machine oil
Biscuit/glaze fire the squares different colours (p. 163).	
(i) Make a simple panel mosaic (p. 167).	
(ii) Make a plaster bed mosaic (p. 168).	
(iii) Fix the squares into a design to an existing wall.	Adhesive, spreader
Fill in between them with white or coloured cellulose filler.	Cellulose filler, (paint),
Clean down with a moist sponge.	knife, sponge

5 Clay carving

Use a lump of leather-hard clay. Carve it with any suitable tool.	Craft knife (pen knife, kitchen knife, large nail)
You can burnish it for different surface effect.	Knife, spoon or fork handle (toothbrush handle, bone folder)
Handle it with care: the clay is unfired. If the model is not too heavy or thick you could, with precautions, fire it; though there would be an element of risk in this owing to the uncertain consistency of the clay.	

COKE, COAL

1 Coke and coal relief

Crumble coke or coal (or both) into a gritty dust.	Hammer
Make a glued relief (p. 166). Use the contrasting qualities of coke and coal and the plain or coloured panel to make your design.	
You can use other materials of a similar nature with the coke and coal.	(Sand, stone dust, slate dust, brick dust, building block dust, clinker dust, bird-cage grit, glitter, metal filings, rust dust, sawdust, chalk dust)

2 Coal (and chippings) mosaic

Break up the coal into small squarish pieces. Use the coal with a contrasting material.	Hammer Granite chippings, marble chippings, gravel
(i) Make a simple panel mosaic (p. 167).	
(ii) Make a plaster bed mosaic (p. 168).	

CONSTRUCTION PAPER see Sugar Paper (U.K.)

CORK AND CORKS

1 Rough cork study

Make a study of the natural patterns and textures in rough cork, using any suitable material or process.

Materials, tools as needed

2 Rough cork relief

Assemble naturally shaped pieces of cork to make a flat shape or a design. Make any change in the shapes with as little cutting as possible.

Make a simple panel relief (p. 167).

If you use hardboard, masonite or insulation board as a panel, fix the cork with glue, thread or fine wire. For threading or wiring, pierce through the cork and board in inconspicuous places with an awl or fine drill. Pass the thread or wire through them and fasten it out of sight behind.

Craft knife

If you use a wood panel, fix the cork as above, or with fine screws or panel pins. Countersink any screw heads that show, and fill in with small pieces of cork and glue.

3 Rough cork construction

Assemble naturally shaped pieces of cork to make a standing, hanging or projecting form. Trim them if needed to fit together better, but cut as little as possible. Wire them together as they are by piercing the cork first with an awl or drill. Twist the wire out of sight. Or make a simple framework of battens, wood strips or wood blocks. Fix them to it, using glue, screws, panel pins or finishing nails—for front or all-round viewing.

Craft knife

Wire, pliers, awl (wood drill)
Battens, (wood blocks), nails, hammer, saw
Adhesive, spreader or
Screws, awl (wood drill), screwdriver or Panel pins, or finishing nails, hammer

4 Cork collage/relief

Cut up cork tiles or cork floor covering into various shapes. Use differences of colour or texture for contrast.
Make a collage (p. 165) or simple panel relief (p. 167).

Craft knife

5 Cork mosaic

Cut up cork tiles or cork floor covering into different sized squares. Use differences of colour or texture for contrast.
(i) Make a simple panel mosaic (p. 167).
(ii) Make a plaster skimmed panel mosaic (p. 170).

Craft knife

6 Cork print

Prepare a flat cork collage or mosaic, 4, 5.
(i) Make a roll-through print (p. 176).
(ii) Ink and make a print (p. 175).

See 4, 5

7 Cork rubbing

a Make a rubbing of the rough cork (p. 179).
You can tear out and assemble different rubbings to make a collage (p. 165).

b Make a rubbing (p. 179) of any cork collage or mosaic you have made that will give an impression.

8 Bottle cork relief

Use corks as they are, or cut into sections across, lengthwise or diagonally.
Arrange them with either face upwards.
(i) Make a simple panel relief (p. 167).
(ii) Make a plaster skimmed panel relief (p. 170).

Craft knife

9 Bottle cork print

Use corks as they are, or cut into them in some way.
Make a pattern of prints (p. 175).

Craft knife

CORRUGATED CARDBOARD

1 Corrugated cardboard collage

Cut a sheet of corrugated cardboard into various shapes.
(You may find two or three colours of sheeting.)
Arrange the shapes with the corrugations lying in different directions to make a surface of contrasting light and shadow effect.
Make a collage (p. 165).

Craft knife (scissors)

2 Corrugated cardboard relief

a Cut a sheet of corrugated cardboard into strips, some short, some longer; some narrow, some wider.
Roll some of the strips with the corrugations inside, some with them outside. Use a paper clip to stop them unrolling.
Cut a shape of firm cardboard or board.
Glue a small area and stick one of the rolls *on end* to it.
Do the same with another roll next to it. Glue them where they meet.
Carry on in this way, arranging the different sizes of roll to most effect. Fix some spirals tight; let others unwind a little before fixing. The design will depend on how you space, join or interlock them.

Craft knife (scissors)

Paper clips.

Cardboard (board, saw)
Adhesive, spreader

b Cut up a sheet of corrugated cardboard into flat pieces.
Bend, curve or roll them to make different shapes, cutting into them if needed.
Arrange these shapes and stick them to a base of firm cardboard or board as a high modelled relief. Use the contrast of plain and corrugated sides.

Craft knife (scissors)

Cardboard (board, saw)
Adhesive, spreader

3 Corrugated cardboard construction

Cut a sheet of corrugated cardboard into flat pieces.
Bend, curve or roll them to make different shapes, cutting into them if needed.
Combine and assemble them into a standing, hanging or projecting form, using the contrast of plain and corrugated sides. Glue them together, making sure each one adheres before going on to the next.
You may need to support some of the forms with stouter cardboard or other suitable materials.

Craft knife (scissors)

Adhesive, spreader
Cardboard, board, wood,
wire with necessary tools

4 Corrugated cardboard plaster relief

Make a corrugated cardboard collage (1).
Make a plaster cast of it (p. 174).
The plaster relief will have the corrugations in reverse.
You can colour it (p. 173). Let the colour flood the corrugations to produce their own contrasts of tone.

See above, 1

5 Corrugated cardboard rubbing

a Make a corrugated cardboard collage (1) or a corrugated cardboard plaster relief (4).
Make a rubbing (p. 179).

See above, 1
See above, 4

b Use a small shape of corrugated cardboard.
On the same piece of printing paper, make a number of overlapping rubbings, turning the cardboard in various ways to make a design.

Craft knife (scissors)

6 Corrugated cardboard print

a Make a corrugated cardboard collage (1) or a corrugated cardboard plaster relief (4).
(i) Make a roll-through print (p. 176).
(ii) Ink it and make a print (p. 175).

See above, 1
See above, 4

b Use a small shape of corrugated cardboard.   Craft knife (scissors)
(i) On the same piece of printing paper, make a num-
number of overlapping roll-through prints (p.176) turning the cardboard in various ways to make a design.
(ii) Doing the same, ink and print the cardboard
(p. 175).
In both 5 and 6 the corrugated cardboard will tend to
flatten fairly soon, so the rubbings or prints you can
make from it will be limited.

CURTAIN RINGS

1 Curtain ring relief

Use different sized curtain rings, together with any
other suitably shaped objects. They can be spaced out,   (Beads, buttons, counters,
touching, overlapping, or built up in tiers.   tube tops, washers, nuts,
(i) Make a simple panel relief (p. 167).   small shapes of metal
(ii) Make a plaster skimmed panel relief (p. 170).   gauze or screening)

2 Curtain ring print

Make a *flat* design of curtain rings (1).   See above, 1
(i) Make a roll-through print (p. 176).
(ii) Ink it and make a print (p. 175).

3 Curtain ring appliqué

Use different sized curtain rings, together with any
other suitably shaped objects.   See above, 1
Stretch a piece of fabric over a frame by long stitches   Frame, fabric
behind, or with staples.
Sew the rings and other pieces to it in a design. They   Thread, needle
can be spaced out, touching, overlapping, or built up   Staple gun
in tiers.
(Things like counters can be sewn by stitching across
them in different directions a few times.)

CUTTLEFISH BONE

You can get this from a pet food shop.

1 Cuttlefish carving

The cuttlefish bone should be firm, not crumbly.
Carve it in the hands with any small tool that seems   Craft knife (penknife,
suitable. You can get quite fine details with the right   nail file, nail, darning
one.   needle)

Mount the carving for safety:
To mount it in the round, nail up through the centre of a small wood block. Drill up into the cuttlefish with a fine drill the same size as the nail. Glue the nail and lower the bone onto it.

Nail, hammer, wood block, drill, adhesive, spreader

To mount it in relief, cut, score and bend a suitably coloured cardboard to stand as a screen. Or just cut out · a shape of card to pin up or hang. Glue the bone to it.

Craft knife, cardboard, adhesive, spreader

2 Cuttlefish modelling

Carve the cuttlefish bone as the main part of a form.

Carving tools, see above, 1

Add other materials to complete the form by inserting them into drilled holes or slots and fixing them there with glue.

Other materials, e.g. paper, plastic, beads, thread, fine wire, feathers, with necessary tools
Drill, craft knife, adhesive, spreader

Mount the model as above (1).

Mounting tools, see above, 1

3 Cuttlefish mosaic

Scale off small fragments of the bone.
Use them with any other light materials for contrast.

Craft knife
(Scale fragments of pearl shell, slate, Honesty seed pod, onion peel, tree bark)

Make a simple panel mosaic (p. 167).

DRIFTWOOD

Use driftwood that the sea has shaped and textured and bleached.

1 Driftwood study

Make a study of the shape, colour and texture of driftwood, using any suitable material or process.

Materials, tools as needed

2 Driftwood relief

Select different pieces of wood with a contrast of shape, colour or texture.
Re-shape any that you need to.

Make a simple panel relief (p. 167).
It may be possible to fix the wood by screwing through from the back of the panel into it. (Planed wood can be a sympathetic mount for the weathered driftwood). You could use other kinds of beach salvage with the driftwood.

Saw, craft knife, pen-knife, chisel, gouge, (mallet), spokeshave, surform, sandpaper, bench vice, clamp, G-cramp

(Cork, rope, trawl net, rusted metal, shell, pebble, dried seaweed, encrusted concrete, debris)

3 Driftwood carving

The driftwood should be dry.
From the shapes and textures already present in the wood, carve a more defined shape.
If the wood is soft and only needs whittling, carve it in the hands. If it is harder and needs a variety of tools, set it up in a bench vice or clamp.
Saw off large unwanted parts first.
Work round the wood, reducing it with the best tool for each stage, until you have brought out the shape you want. Finish with sandpaper if you want it smooth. A final wax polish can sometimes enhance the wood, though the quality of the dry wood itself may be best left alone.
If you are mounting it, drill, dowel and glue the foot into a heavier wood block.

Or screw and bracket it to project from a wall or vertical panel.

Tools, as above, 2

Wax polish, cloth
Wood drill, dowelling, wood block, adhesive, spreader
Bracket, screws, awl, (wood drill). screwdriver
Rawlplugs, punch and hammer, or masonry drill (wood panel, saw)

Driftwood construction. Child

Driftwood carving

4 Driftwood construction

Select various shapes of driftwood.
Assemble them into a standing, hanging or projecting
form, re-shaping any parts you need to.

Tools, as above, 2

Secure some of the main pieces to each other with
screws or bolts and nuts, depending on size and weight.
Drill the wood first.

Screws, awl (wood drill),
screwdriver
or
Nuts, bolts, wood drill,
spanner

Add further pieces in the same way. The construction
should be rigid and secure at each stage.
You could use other kinds of beach salvage with the
driftwood as above, 2.
Mount the finished work, as above, 3.

(Other salvage)

5 Driftwood–as a mount

Select a piece of driftwood with natural 'pockets' in it
(hollows, holes).
Find interesting pebbles or similar objects that could
fit the pockets.

Pebble, weathered glass,
shell, chalk

Shape the pockets more accurately to house the objects.
Smooth the wood down if needed. Fix the objects into
place with gum or glue.

Craft knife, pen knife,
chisel, gouge, sandpaper
Adhesive, spreader

Mount the driftwood on a suitably surfaced panel,
using glue or screws.

Board (wood), saw

As in 2, it may be possible to fix the wood by screwing
through from the back of the panel into it.

Screws, awl (wood drill),
screwdriver

6 Driftwood painting

Paint the different surfaces of driftwood:

Powder paint (emulsion
paint, house oil paint–
primer needed here)

To emphasise and bring them out.
To give the shape a new character.
To decorate the shape.
First smooth any of the surfaces if needed.

Sandpaper

7 Driftwood rubbing

Make a rubbing of the driftwood (p. 179).

EGG BOXES

These come in many different kinds of interesting shape nowadays.
Other well-mould containers can be used in a similar way, or in conjunction with the egg boxes, e.g. apple and other fruit separators, sweet or candy separators.

1 Egg box relief

Cut and trim egg boxes to fit, either way up, as a relief. They can be side by side, spaced out, or built up in various ways.
Make a simple panel relief (p. 167).
The wells can be decorated in different ways:
Paint or spray them.

Line them with other materials.

Fill them with other objects.

Combine any of these.

Craft knife (scissors)

Powder paint, (emulsion paint, paint aerosol, spray)

Tissue, fabric, metal foil, texturing material with adhesive
Pebble, shell, glass, wood, machine part, plastic—
with adhesive

Chocolate separator relief

2 Egg box construction

Cut and trim egg boxes to assemble as a standing, hanging or projecting construction. Include other boxes or cardboard if needed.

Stick them together one at a time, making sure each has stuck well before adding more.
You can decorate the finished shape in different ways as above, 1, though in some cases it may be better to anticipate their effect in the over-all design and do this first.

Craft knife (scissors)

(Other boxes, cardboard)

Adhesive, spreader

See above, 1

3 Egg box plaster cast

Cut and trim egg boxes to fit side by side and form a mould, all the same way up.
Glue them to board.
Build a retaining cardboard wall round them. Fasten it with a staple or paper clip.
Make a plaster cast (p. 174).
Colour the cast if needed (p. 174).

Craft knife (scissors)

Adhesive, spreader
Board, saw
Cardboard, stapler
(paper clip)

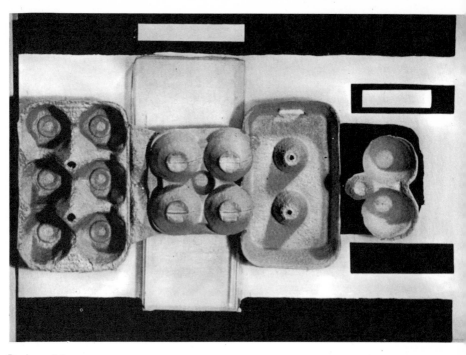

Egg box relief

Egg shell relief

EGG SHELLS

Making an egg shell mosaic

Egg shell mosaic (detail). Student

1 Egg shell mosaic

Clean the shells and separate the different colours.
Break them into small pieces.
Use the different colours of shell, and either side of
them.
Make a simple panel mosaic (p. 167).
Glue small areas of the panel at a time, and transfer the
pieces to it, fitting them close together or spacing them
a little apart. The occasional larger piece that shatters
under pressure will still stick, and it will provide an
interesting contrast of grouping. Alternatively, you can
glue the egg shell pieces separately and fix them down.

2 Egg shell relief

Use half egg shells. Clean them and trim them with
small scissors (nail scissors are useful). Cut slowly to
avoid breaking the edges too much.

Small scissors

(i) Make a simple panel relief (p. 167), using the shells
either way up. Stick all meeting surfaces.
(ii) Use a rigid container about the height of half a
shell and wide enough to hold a number of them side
by side. Any shape will do. (You may prefer to make
one up yourself. See plaster bed reliefs, p. 168.)

Stout cardboard box lid
(wholesale biscuit or
candy tin lid)

Glue the shells, by their ends chiefly, into the container,
and glue any sides that meet each other.

Adhesive, spreader

Mix some plaster (p. 172). It should pour easily.
Put it in a jug and pour it so that it floods in between
all the shells and rises to the top of the container. When
it has set, break or nip off with tweezers any edges of
shell that show above it. Or remove the shells, just
leaving their cast impression.

Jug

Tweezers

Colour the plaster if needed (p. 173), though the play of
light over the white surfaces should be interesting in
itself.

FABRIC

1 Fabric collage

Cut shapes from different fabrics:
dress, curtain, upholstery and general furnishing
fabric, butter muslin or cheesecloth, hessian or burlap,
unbleached calico, monks cloth, linen scrim, linen
crash, linen towelling, linen dishcloth, open-mesh linen
dishcloth, cambric, calpreta, buckram, spun cotton,
pillow cotton, cotton crash, cotton curtain net, speckled
(cotton) crash, cotton piqué, waxed balloon cloth,
house cloth, soft linen tailoring canvas, deckchair canvas, rayon crash, vilene, honeycomb towelling, silk,
suede, organdie, corduroy, soft leather, synthetic fibres,
American oil cloth, embroidery fabric.

Make a collage (p. 165), using colour and texture contrasts, together with any other related materials you
may wish to include.

Scissors

(Sequins, buttons, cord,
thread, lace edging, fur
scraps, beads, feathers,
cheap jewellery)

2 Fabric appliqué

Fabric appliqué. Student

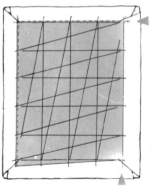

Fabric stretched over panel

Cut shapes from different fabrics (see above).
Arrange them into a design.

Cut another piece of fabric–a stiffer kind preferably,
like hessian or monks cloth–making it 1″ or so larger
all round than your design. Sew the fabric shapes on it,
catching them round the edges, and leaving the border
clear. Keep it flat at all times, and don't let the stitching
bunch it. The stitches can blend with the fabric or
make a definite pattern on it.

Cut a panel of board the same shape as your design
area. Lay the appliqué on it, fold the edges round the
back, and staple, or sew them with long crossing
stitches to each other, pulling the design taut.

Alternatively, you can start with the stretched fabric
stapled or sewn over an old picture frame (or a frame
you have made up). Cut and arrange fabric pieces into
a design to fit it, and sew them on.

Scissors

Thread, needle

Board, saw

Staple gun

Frame (battens with
panel pins, or light nails,
hammer, saw, or other
tools as needed)

3 Fabric weaving

Get some netting or similar mesh.

Strawberry netting
(fish net, open-weave
curtain net, netted duster,
rug canvas)

Have it flat, or hanging taut (weight the bottom edge, if needed).

(Small weights)

Cut different kinds of fabric (see above) into long thin strips. Using a safety pin or a piece of bent wire, weave them across the netting, selecting strips that combine to make a pattern. Catch any ends with a stitch or two to prevent them slipping out of place.

Scissors
Safety pin (wire)

Thread, needle

4 Fabric rubbing/print

Cut shapes from different fabrics with a 'hard' texture.

Scissors
Hessian, scrim, net,
dishcloth

Arrange them into a design (no overlapping preferably) and make a collage (p. 165).
When it is quite dry:
(i)   Make a rubbing (p. 179).
(ii) Make a roll-through print (p. 176).
(iii) Ink it and make a print (p. 175).

5 Fabric as a painting surface

Cut a panel of board or wood.

Board (wood), saw

Cut a piece of suitably textured fabric for painting on— 1″ or so larger all round than the panel.

Scissors

Glue the panel and lay the fabric down on it, pressing outwards from the centre to expel any air pockets. Turn over the edges and stick them down behind. (If you trim the overlapping corners off diagonally first, it will save the turned-over fabric from bunching there.)

Scotch glue, brush,
glue pot

Alternatively, stretch a fairly closely woven fabric over a frame (or a stretcher specially made for this). Turn the edges over and tack or staple them to the reverse side. To do this, fix at the four points opposite each other, i.e. north and south, east and west, pulling the fabric taut but without straining it (this could distort the weave). Now continue fixing at points diagonally opposite each other. Turn the corners over and fix them down.

Frame (stretcher)
Tacks, hammer (staple gun)

When you have stuck or stretched the fabric, mix some size (according to the instructions on the packet) and brush it on the fabric. As the size dries, the fabric on a frame or stretcher will tighten.

Size, broad brush, pan

You can now give this a coat of emulsion paint or builders' undercoat if you are going to paint in oils.

Emulsion paint (builders'
undercoat)

6 Fabric as a tool

Screw up a small piece of fabric, dip it in paint, and use it instead of a brush as a painting tool. You get different effects by using it in different ways—dabbing, sweeping, rotating, stroking.

7 Fabric tie dye

Use any length of plain fabric (a thin cotton fabric is good to start with).

Gather up different parts of the fabric with thread or string by tying small objects into it; by bunching and binding tightly; or by catching at them with long or short stitches.

Thread (string)
Scissors
Pebble, button, nut
(either kind), large bead,
bottle cork
or
Thread, needle

(What you are doing, of course, is tying parts of the fabric away from the dye.)

Mix a cold or hot water dye (a solution of permanganate of potash will do to start with). Dip the fabric in for the required period. Take it out and untie the thread or string—or take out the stitches. You will have a variety of patterns depending on how you gathered the fabric up.

Cold or hot water dye, bowl

If you have used a fast dye, you can now wash and iron the fabric. (A little salt in the dye helps its fastness).

Flat iron

8 Fabric wax resist

See under Candle or Wax (p. 22, 139).

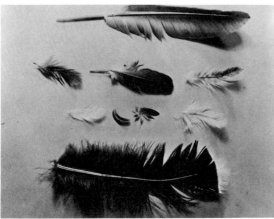

FEATHERS

1 Feather study

Make a study of the shape, colour, pattern and texture of a feather, using any suitable material or process.

Materials, tools as needed

2 Feather collage

Select different kinds of feathers and arrange them into a design to create movements of colour and texture.
Make a collage (p. 165).

Spread a *clear* adhesive on the card thinly, one part at a time, and transfer the feathers to it. Press them down gently under a clean piece of paper to avoid getting your hands sticky.

Paper

3 Feather impression

Prepare a clay slab for making impressions (p. 163).
Use firm, sharply defined feathers. Press them into the
clay under a stiff piece of cardboard to make a design   Cardboard
of spaced, touching or overlapping shapes. Lift each
feather off carefully afterwards.
(i) Biscuit/glaze fire the slab (p. 163) or
(ii) Make a plaster cast of it (p. 174).
Colour the cast if needed (p. 174).

4 Feather print

a Lay a firm, sharply defined feather on a board.   Board
Make a roll-through print (p. 176).
Move the feather a little underneath and repeat the
print process.
Do this a number of times to make a multiple design of
the feather.

b Make a feather collage (2) without overlapping too   See above, 2
much.
(i) Make a roll-through print (p. 176).
(ii) Ink it and make a print (p. 175) if the feathers are
firm enough.

5 Feather – other uses

a Use a feather for 'feathered' marbling.
b Use a stiff feather quill for ink drawing. Cut the   Craft knife
point obliquely with a sharp craft knife.

Feather print

FELT

1 Felt collage

Use different coloured felts. Cut them into various   Scissors
shapes.
Make a collage (p. 165).
You may wish to use a contrasting fabric with the felt.   (Another fabric)

2 Felt appliqué

Use different coloured felts. Cut them into various   Scissors
shapes.
Stretch another piece of fabric over a frame, turning   Frame
the edges over and stapling them, or pulling them taut   Staple gun (thread,
with long crossing stitches at the back.   needle)

Arrange a design of felt shapes on it and sew them in place by catching with short stitches. The shapes can be spaced out, touching or overlapping.

You may wish to use a contrasting fabric with the felt.   (Another fabric)

3 Felt modelling

Use different coloured felts.

a Make a drawing of a simple model.   Drawing medium, paper

(i) With soft felt, work out the shapes of its different sides and make a sewing pattern for them, allowing extra at the edges for turning in.

Cut the side panels out and sew them with a running   Scissors, thread, needle
stitch, leaving part of one panel open. Turn it inside out and pack it with any suitable material.   Kapok (cotton wool,
foam plastic pieces,
Sew up the last panel.   old stockings)

Sew on any similarly modelled or flat pieces you need   (Sequins, buttons, cord,
to complete the form, together with any additional   beads, feathers, cheap
materials.   jewellery, other fabric)

(ii) With thicker felt, cut the pattern to size and sew   Equipment and materials,
the panels together (right side facing out) with a small   as above (i)
running stitch or overstitch, leaving part of one panel open. Then complete as above, i.

b Cut out felt shapes and assemble them freely as they   Scissors
are to make a form. Fold or gather them as needed, and
secure them by sewing or glueing.   Thread, needle
or
Adhesive, spreader

4 Felt–other uses

a Use as an inking pad in print making (left-over scraps will be useful for this). Cut the felt to the shape
of a tin can lid, and soak it in ink or dye when you are   Tin can lid
ready to use it.

b Use it as a bright contrasting fabric in other collage work or in reliefs and flat plaster casts.

FILM

Use old or unwanted film strip and negatives.

1 Film mosaic

Cut up the film strip or negatives into different sized   Craft knife (scissors)
squares.

Arrange them into a design, using the different sizes, tones and colours.

Make a simple panel mosaic (p. 167).

2 Film collage

Cut up the film strip or negatives into different shapes. Arrange them freely into a design, using the different shapes, tones and colours.
Make a collage (p. 165).

Craft knife (scissors)

3 Film etch

Cut two equal squares of film strip or negative that will fit into a projector slide mount (usually $2'' \times 2''$).
Engrave a design on each with a sharp point. The designs can correspond with each other, but they need not.
Insert them together in a slide mount, and project onto a screen or light wall. Your 'etching' will project as a white line design. (The reason for using two squares of film is to cancel out any images present on them. And the doubling-up produces interesting effects.)

Craft knife (scissors)

Divider (compass, nail, bodkin, awl)

Slide mount
Projector (screen)

FISHBONES

1 Fishbone relief

Clean the fishbones thoroughly.
Arrange them into a design of spaced, touching or overlapping shapes.
(i)   Make a simple panel relief (p. 167).
(ii) Make a plaster skimmed panel relief (p. 170).

2 Fishbone impression

Prepare a clay slab for making impressions (p. 163).
Press the fishbones into the clay under a stiff piece of cardboard to make a design of spaced, touching or overlapping shapes. Lift each bone off carefully afterwards.
(i)   Biscuit/glaze fire the slab (p. 163) or
(ii) Make a plaster cast of it (p. 174).
Colour the cast if needed (p. 174).

Cardboard

3 Fishbone combing

Use a suitable fishbone for combing a pattern in paint or in a marbling medium.
a Damp and stretch a sheet of paper by fixing it with gum strip to a board. Cover it with a coat of powder paint mixed with paste.

Draw the fish bone through it in different directions to make a design.

Board, paper, sponge, gum strip, (U.S.: Scotch tape)
Powder paint, paste, bowl, flat brush

b Fill a large flat dish with water.

Drip a mixture of special marbling medium or oil paint and turps onto the water. Draw the fishbone through it in different directions to create a design of colour movements.

Lay a sheet of paper flat on the water and lift it off cleanly, picking up the marbled design on the under-side.

Dish
Marbling medium (oil paint with turps), brush

Paper

FOAM PLASTIC

You can use foam plastic in several ways in connection with other crafts.

In print making

a As an inking pad.

Cut a shape of foam plastic to fit a tin can or plastic lid. Soak it in ink, dye or powder paint. Use it for printing small objects or blocks.

Tin can lid (plastic lid)
Scissors
Ink (dye, powder paint)

b As a deep printing blanket.

Cut a shape of foam plastic to lie over an uneven surface block, e.g. a sand and wire relief. Roller over the foam, pressing the printing paper underneath into all the depressions. See p. 176.

Scissors

c To make a deep printing roller.

Cut a strip of foam plastic the width of an ordinary roller, and enough to wrap round it several times, depending on thickness. Glue it along the edge at start and finish. This will pad out the roller so that it will ink into all the depressions of the block.

Scissors
Roller
Adhesive, spreader

In painting

Cut foam plastic and fold it into a small compact wad. Keep the shape with a strong elastic band.

You can paint with this, held as it is or fixed to an improvised handle.

Scissors
Elastic band
Piece of wood, wire, etc.

In modelling

Use foam plastic in sheets or small pieces to pad out soft models (toys, puppets, soft sculpture).

Scissors

FORMICA

Break up formica into irregular pieces with a suitable tool, or saw it into regular pieces.
Breaking may cause the formica to flake on one side or the other, but you can limit this with care.
If you need to drill formica, use a metal drill.

Pliers, pincers, mosaic cutter, bradawl and hammer, handsaw, hacksaw, metal drill

1 Formica mosaic

Using the different colours and patterns available in formica, break or cut up a few pieces into small shapes.
(i)   Make a simple panel mosaic (p. 167).
(ii) Make a plaster skimmed panel mosaic (p. 170).

Tools, see above

2 Formica relief

Using the different colours and patterns available in formica, break or cut it up into various shapes.
(i)   Make a simple panel relief (p. 167).
(ii) Make a plaster skimmed panel relief (p. 170).

Tools, see above

3 Formica print

Use formica to make a monoprint (p. 177).

Tools, see above

4 Formica construction

Using the different colours and patterns available in formica, break or cut it into shapes and assemble them to make a standing, hanging or projecting construction. Glue the parts together and reinforce the joins behind with wood strips or blocks if needed (balsa wood will do for small models). Wait till one part of the assembly has set well before adding the next.

Tools, see above

Adhesive, spreader

Wood strip (wood block), with tools needed

5 Formica–other uses

a As an inking plate for print making.

b As a painting surface. You may need to prime it first with emulsion paint.

Emulsion paint

c As support for a drawing block. You just need a clip then.

Foldback clip
(bulldog clip)

d As a surface for pouring plaster on for a plaster engraving or print.

FURNITURE

Use any unwanted broken furniture from the home, school or office. This is often to be had just by rescuing it from an attic, boiler room or basement—or by a visit to a junk shop or a job-lot auction.

1 Furniture relief

Use flat shaped pieces of furniture as they are, or cut down and re-shaped:
chair seat (plywood, perforated, cane), occasional and card table tops, drawer panels, small doors from cabinets and dressers—especially carved, beaded or embossed ones, veneered panels of all kinds, carved or covered screens, picture frames, thinly shaped legs, arms and backs, upholstery materials . . . the list is almost endless, of course.
Make a simple panel relief (p. 167).

Other tools you may need: chisel, mallet, plane, surform, sandpaper

2 Furniture carving

Use suitably shaped pieces of furniture that in themselves perhaps suggest a starting point for a carving:
rounded legs of an old table, sideboard or dresser,

Wood carving. Adult

shaped parts of bannisters, balusters, plant pot stands
—or flatter pieces, see above, 1, for relief carving.

An idea may come from handling the wood, and you
can carve directly to bring out the form you see in it;
or you may wish to sketch out first on paper the form
you want, and work from that.

Drawing medium, paper

Set the wood up in a vice, or with bench screws or
G-cramps (C clamps), and carve with any suitable tool.
Much of this wood will be very hard, and you will want
good cutting edges (see Wood, p. 143).

Tools, see Wood

3 Furniture construction

Assemble suitable pieces of furniture as they are, or cut
down and re-shaped, to make a standing, hanging or
projecting form.

Tools, see above

Fix the main parts together first and build the other
parts on. You will probably find it best to use dowels
for this (drill meeting parts), or screws (drill the wood
first where possible). Countersink the screw heads and
fill in with plastic wood (U.K. Brummer stopping).
Glue any meeting surfaces as well to make sure of a
good join.

You can use the colour of the wood itself, or paint the
construction at any suitable stage.

Dowelling, wood drill
or
Screws, wood drill,
countersink, awl,
screwdriver, plastic wood
(Brummer stopping)
Adhesive, spreader
Emulsion paint (house oil
paint)

4 Furniture print

Use suitable flat pieces of wood from old furniture to
make woodcut prints (see Wood off-cuts, p. 146).

5 Furniture—other uses

a As a panel (often already 'primed') for painting on
in emulsion or oil paint.

b As a panel for mounting a mosaic or relief.

GLASS

Be careful in handling glass, not only of the main piece
you are working with, but of the small waste fragments
and powdered glass that can so easily be overlooked.

Use clear or coloured glass.

Different kinds of clear glass:
window, mirror, dimpled, reeded, frosted, plate, reinforced, bottle.

Different kinds of coloured glass:
antique (potmetal colours), bottle—beer, liqueur, wine,
cleaning fluid, medicine bottles like milk of magnesia;
decorative bowls and vases, coffee jars.

Weathered glass found washed up on beaches is both safe and beautiful.

NB *Much of this glass is being replaced by plastics of various kinds. It is worth saving as much as you can while it is still around. The sources of such cheap coloured glass may be running dry.*

To cut glass, make sure the glass is clean and dry, and work on a flat surface. Use a wheel or diamond cutter. For flat pieces, mark where you want to cut (a fibre tip pen is useful for this) and lay a straight edge along the line. Draw the cutter once across the glass with gentle but firm pressure. Put a matchstick under one end of the cut and apply a little downward pressure on both sides of it. The glass should break clean. For curved pieces, keep the glass and the cutter steady while you do it.

Glass cutter

Fibre tip pen
Straight edge
Matchstick

To break up glass. Protect the eyes and wear leather gloves and an apron. Wrap the glass in thick sacking and work on a board or stone floor if possible.

Protective clothing
Sacking, board, mallet
(hammer)

1 Glass mosaic/relief

Use fairly flat pieces of glass for these, though chunkier pieces can be used in some.

Cut or break up the glass into small, regular pieces, or a variety of freer shapes of any size.

Tools, see above

(i)   Make a simple panel mosaic or relief (p. 167).

(ii) Make a plaster bed mosaic or relief (p. 168).

(iii) Make a mosaic or relief using the reversing process (p. 170). If the pieces are not flat here, the plaster, cement mix, fondu or resin that you are backing them with may tend to flow under them, and they will not be showing clearly when you reverse the panel.

(iv) Make a window mosaic or relief by sticking the pieces to a sheet of glass (or a window), using a clear glue or laminating resin, 1 oz resin : 6 drops hardener. You can draw a design of the main shapes lightly on glass with a felt pen first if needed, or work directly without a predrawn design.

Glass sheet
Glue (resin and hardener)

Felt pen

If you are working on a vertical surface you may need to fix the lowest pieces first and work upwards, giving each level time to set off before going up to the next.

2 Glass window model

a Cut a corresponding window in two pieces of stout cardboard or board.

Cardboard, craft knife
(board, fret saw)

The glass area will be a little bigger than the window. Cut a few glass shapes and lay them within the area. Cut more pieces to make a second layer, lying over parts of the first. Fix them with small beads of glue, or resin and hardener (see above). Do the same again until all spaces between glass pieces have been covered by further glass.

Glass cutter

Glue (resin and hardener)

Glue the assembled glass between the boards.

Cut a strip of manilla the width of the two boards and glass together. Glue it round the edges of the boards to finish off neatly.

Colour the boards if needed.

Manilla, craft knife
(scissors)
Adhesive, spreader
Powder paint (emulsion paint)

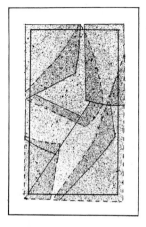 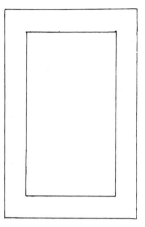

Arrangement of glass pieces

b Arrange a few pieces of glass in an interesting relationship (not too big).

For each piece of glass, shape two wads of clay or plasticine, ½″ deep, and a little smaller all round than their piece of glass. Press them on front and back to make a sandwich of the glass, which should then be showing about ¼″ round the edges.

Glass cutter

Clay (plasticine)

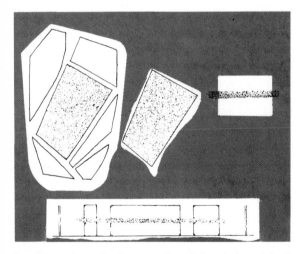

Glass between clay wads

Lay the pieces back on a board in their original arrangement, a little clear of each other.

Cut a cardboard wall the height of the sandwiches and set it up round them about 1″ away, and curved to any shape that encloses them well. Fix it with paper clips and press clay round the bottom edge to seal it.

Mix plaster of Paris (p. 172).

Pour it in, making sure it floods into all parts until it rises level with the top of the clay wads.

When the plaster is set, remove the walls and the clay wads from the glass. The glass areas will now be clear.

Sandpaper and colour the plaster if needed (p. 173).

Board

Cardboard, craft knife (scissors)
Paper clips

Jug

Sandpaper

NB If you will need a supporting stand for the finished model, set wire rods into place through the cardboard wall before pouring the plaster in. They can be made to stand as they are, or to fix into a base of wood or plaster.

Wire rod, hacksaw, awl

Wood or plaster block, drill

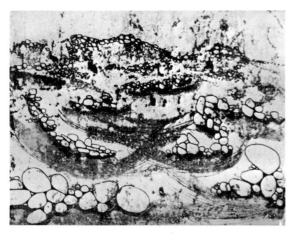

Monoprint from glass. Student

3 Glass – other uses

a Use plate glass (or window glass if it is safe to do so) as an inking plate for print making, or as a surface for monoprinting.

Monoprint from glass

b Use plate glass (or window glass if it is safe to do so) for pouring plaster on when you want to make a plaster engraving or print.

HARDBOARD (MASONITE)

Hardboard is tough, light and rigid. It is about $\frac{1}{8}''$ thick, and is supplied in large sheets (usually $8' \times 4'$) or in smaller off-cuts.

There are other kinds of board known as insulation (or pin) board. This is strong though softer in texture. It is about $\frac{1}{2}''$ thick and is also supplied in large sheets or off-cuts.
You can use either of these boards in the following jobs.

1 Hardboard (Masonite)–as a painting surface

You can paint on the board as it is with powder or emulsion paint, though you have a better surface if you size it or give it a coat of emulsion paint first.

Size, bowl, broad brush (emulsion paint, broad brush or paint roller)

If you are going to paint in oil, you should prepare the board first as above, or with size followed by builders' undercoat.

(Builders' undercoat)

There is also a white primer on the market for this.

(White primer)

You can also make up many pleasant surfaces to work on by glueing different kinds of fabric to the board (see list under Fabric). Cut the shape of hardboard you want. Cut a piece of fabric 1" or so bigger all round. Glue the board all over and lay the fabric on it, pressing it out from the centre to expel any air pockets and coax any creases to the edge. (Iron badly creased fabric first.) If you are using butter muslin or cheesecloth, or a similar thin fabric, work it out flat with a glue brush: the glue comes through! Cut off the corners diagonally a little way from the board. Turn the edges of the fabric over and glue them down behind.

Saw
Fabric, scissors
Scotch glue, brush, glue pot

When the glue has dried you can prepare the fabric for painting on by any of the ways suggested above for hardboard.

Yet another way of preparing an interesting surface is to glue the board, or paint it thickly with emulsion paint, and cover it liberally with sand or a similar material.

See above
Scotch glue, broad brush, glue pot
or
Emulsion paint, broad brush or paint roller

When it has dried, shake off the surplus, go over any bald or thin parts again, and give it a final coat of emulsion paint if you wish.

Sand, stone dust, slate dust, brick dust, building block dust, coal dust, coke dust, clinker dust, bird-cage grit, glitter, sawdust

You can get a similar effect by coating the hardboard with thick emulsion paint and stippling it with the palm of the hand or with a twisted cloth.
Wash all tools and equipment thoroughly as soon as you have finished with them. It is a long business softening a brush or roller that has gone hard with set emulsion or oil paint. And emulsion dries fast!

Cloth

2 Hardboard (Masonite) relief

Cut several shapes of hardboard (or peg board). Sandpaper the edges.
Arrange them either side up to make a design.
Make a simple panel relief (p. 167).

Saw, sandpaper

3 Hardboard (Masonite) construction

Cut shapes of hardboard (or peg board) to assemble

into a standing, hanging or projecting construction. Sandpaper the edges.

Make any central supports of battens or wood blocks that you need, and glue, nail or screw the hardboard shapes to them, and to each other, in the order that seems best. If you do not need any supports, just glue the hardboard shapes together.

Saw, sandpaper
Battens or wood strips (wood blocks) with tools
Adhesive, spreader
or
Oval nails (panel pins or finishing nails), hammer
or
Screws, awl (wood drill), screwdriver, countersink

Paint or texture any of the finished construction needed.

Paint, texturing material with adhesive

4 Hardboard (Masonite) print

Cut a shape of hardboard.
a Draw a design on it with sharpened chalk or crayon. Engrave the lines, and texture or pare away any of the areas needed.

Saw
Chalk (crayon)
Linoleum cutter, X-acto gouge, wood gouge, nail, small metal part, hammer

Ink and make a print (p. 175).
The first inking may sink a little (unless you are using a primed board). Later inkings will take better.

b Make a glued relief using sand or similar material (p. 166).
(i) Make a roll-through print (p. 176).
(ii) Ink it and make a print (p. 175).

c Make a design by sticking other materials to it.
(i) Make a roll-through print (p. 176).
(ii) Ink it and make a print (p. 175).
NB This may be an uneven block. See note about this, p. 176.

Adhesive, spreader
Thread, wire, paper, card, coarse fabric

5 Hardboard (Masonite)–other uses

a Use it as an inking plate in print making. Prime the board first with emulsion paint and a coat of house gloss paint–or with a resin-bonded hardboard primer.

Emulsion paint and house gloss paint (hardboard primer)

b Use the perforated pegboard as a panel for hanging tools on. You can get special clips to fit the board for this purpose.

Pegboard clips

JARS

Different kinds of jar lend themselves to different uses: jars for jam, fruit, preserves, pickle, meat extract, paste, coffee and other foods; jars for bath salts and other toilet accessories; jars for industrial and chemical uses. Some are made of clear glass, some of coloured, some of textured glass, some of china.
It is worth saving all shapes and sizes for a while: you will probably find good use for them.

1 A jar as a mount for coloured glass

Use a clear glass jar.

Cut or break coloured or textured glass (*care here!* see Glass, p. 61)–if possible with a curve similar to that of the jar, though this is not essential if the pieces are fairly small. (Some jars are square of course.) Plan an arrangement of the pieces, setting them out flat so that you can transfer them to the upright sides of the jar later to make a 'tower' of transparent colour.

Glass cutter
Sack, mallet, protective clothing

Using a clear glue, or laminating resin and hardener, (1 oz. resin:6 drops hardener) fix them into place, starting from the bottom and working up. Make sure each level has stuck before going on to the next. You can stick them on the inside or the outside of the jar if the curves fit.

Clear adhesive (resin with hardener), spreader

You could glue a number of similar jars together side by side or on top of each other (top to top, bottom to bottom, or top to bottom) to make a screen or tower of colour for standing against the light. If you plan for this, leave the meeting areas clear so that there will be a good join. Glue them in pairs, then glue the pairs together, and so on. Use adhesives as above for this. (Flat sided jars are particularly useful here.)

2 Jars–construction

Use jars that combine to make a well-fitting standing form (probably small or flat sided ones will be best for this). Make a firm arrangement for the base, using adhesives as above, and continue building upwards keeping it well balanced at each stage.

Adhesive, see above

You may find ways of introducing further colour as you go, e.g. with the use of trapped coloured liquids.

Coloured liquid

3 Jars–other uses

a As a water pot.

b As storage for dry or mixed colour (the colours can be seen!).

c As a 'rolling pin' for clay slab work.

LEAVES

'Leaves' here include tree, bush, flower, vegetable and fruit leaves; grasses of all kinds; ferns.

1 Leaf study

Make a study of the shape, colour, pattern and texture of a leaf, using any suitable material or process.

Materials, tools as needed

NB In some of the following jobs you may want your leaves flat. To prepare for this, put them between cards or boards and press them for a day or so under some heavy flat weights, or in a nipping or block press.

Cardboard (boards)
Flat weights (nipping press)

2 Leaf collage

Arrange your leaves into a design using the same or different kinds of leaf.
Make a collage (p. 165).
It may be better to have the leaves flat for this. You can give the collage a different effect by covering it with a single layer of tissue paper (use one or more colours). Lay the paper over the leaves and brush over it evenly with a clear polyurethane varnish or polymer matt medium.

Tissue paper, polyurethane varnish, or polymer matt medium, brush, paraffin, bowl

3 Leaf impression

Prepare a clay slab for making impressions (p. 163).
Use leaves with ridged vein markings or with a pronounced shape:
maple, sycamore, hazel, beech, horse-chestnut, elm, yew, fern.
Lay one or more leaves on the clay in different positions, and press them gently under a piece of stiff cardboard to make a design of the impressions. Lift each leaf off carefully afterwards.
(i) Biscuit/glaze fire the slab (p. 163) or
(ii) Make a plaster cast of it (p. 174).
Colour the cast if needed (p. 174).

Cardboard

4 Grass weaving

Use long flat grasses or reeds. Press them as above.
Use some for warps (up and down) and some for wefts (across).
Arrange the warp grasses on a card or board and pin them at one end.
Weave the other grasses into them.
Trim off any ends clear of your actual weave.
This is not permanent of course. But note under the section on leaf prints and rubbings that you could make further use of this weave.

Cardboard (board), pins

Craft knife (scissors)

Plant print

5 Leaf print

a Place a leaf on a board.
Make a roll-through print (p. 176).
Move the leaf a little and make a second print in the same way through the paper.
Continue doing this until you have an interesting design of spaced, touching or overlapping prints.

Board

b Put out printing ink on an inking plate.
Lay the leaf on some scrap paper and ink it with a roller (on the veined side probably is best). Lay it carefully, ink side down, on a sheet of printing paper. Cover it with a sheet of scrap paper and, holding it still, go over it with a clean roller.
Lift the leaf off cleanly.
Ink and lay it down again on the printing paper in another place and print again.
Continue in this way until you have an interesting design.

Inking plate, printing ink, rollers, printing paper, scrap paper

c Use a well-marked leaf.
Place a sheet of printing paper, at least twice the length of the leaf (longer if possible) on a board.
Ink a leaf, as above, **b**, and lay it, inked side down on the end of the paper nearest you.
Re-charge the roller, and run it straight up over the leaf and on to the paper above. The leaf itself will make an inked print in the lower part, and the roller will carry a 'ghost' image onto the upper part. If your paper is longer, take the roller right to the end with the same movement, carrying fainter ghost images with it as the ink runs out.

Printing paper, board

.See above, b

d Make a leaf collage (2)–without any covering tissue.
(i) Make a roll-through print (p. 176).
(ii) Ink and make a print (p. 175).

See above, 2

e Make a grass weave (4).
(i) Make a roll-through print (p. 176).
(ii) Ink and make a print (p. 175).

See above, 4

6 Leaf rubbing

a Place a well veined leaf on a board.   Board
Make a rubbing (p. 179).
Move the leaf a little and make a second rubbing.
Continue doing this, making a design of the rubbings.

b Make a leaf collage (2).   See above, 2
Make a rubbing of it (p. 179).

c Make a grass weave (4).   See above, 4
Make a rubbing of it (p. 179).

7 Leaf stencil

Put a sheet of paper on a board.   Board, paper, pins
Arrange leaves to make a design on the paper and pin
them down.
With the board lying flat or in an upright position
whichever you find better, spray round the leaves with
ink, dye or thin paint, using a diffuser, blower or an   Ink (dye, paint)
aerosol spray can; or dip a toothbrush in colour and   Diffuser or blower
splatter them (practise this first on a bit of scrap).   (toothbrush, Aerosol spray
You get a different kind of design if you pin on the   can)
leaves one at a time and spray them in succession,   Scrap paper
though you can quickly cover up your first stencils if
you overdo it.
   You could, of course, brush colour on to make your   Brush
stencil. Don't let the ink run under the leaf.

LINOLEUM

The cheapest way to buy linoleum is by the square
yard from a furnishing store. You can then cut it up into
the shapes you want. You can sometimes get off-cuts
even cheaper from the same source, or collect unwanted
trimmings after a lino laying job.
Cut cork linoleum by scoring it with a craft knife and   Craft knife (scissors)
bending it so that it breaks along the line. Then just cut
through the backing. Other kinds of flooring, like vinyl,
can be cut with a craft knife or ordinary household
scissors.

1 Linoleum mosaic

a Use cork lino. This comes in a few different thicknesses and colours.
Cut it into small, squarish shapes.   Craft knife
Using the different shapes, heights and colours:
(i)   Make a simple panel mosaic (p. 167).
(ii) Make a plaster skimmed panel mosaic (p. 170).
You can set the pieces close together or space them

a little apart. Either way, you can fill in between them afterwards with cellulose filler, wiping finally to remove the surplus.

Kitchen knife
Cellulose filler
Sponge (cloth)

b Use the thinner, patterned linoleum (oil cloth, vinyl). Cut into small squarish shapes.
Using the different shapes and colours:
(i) Make a simple panel mosaic (p. 167).
(ii) Make a plaster skimmed panel mosaic (p. 170).

Craft knife (scissors)

2 Linoleum relief

Use either kind of linoleum.

a Cut them into different shapes and sizes.
Using the linoleum flat, or formed in some way by bending:
(i) Make a simple panel relief (p. 167).
(ii) Make a plaster skimmed panel relief (p. 170).

Craft knife (scissors)

b Cut linoleum into narrow strips, not necessarily the same width. Roll them into tight or loose spirals, and arrange them on end to make a design of spiralled and interlocking shapes. Keep them in the rolled position by tying or wiring while you fix them.
(i) Make a simple panel relief (p. 167).
(ii) Make a plaster bed relief (p. 168).

String, scissors (wire, pliers)

3 Linoleum inlay

Use the thicker cork linoleum.
Cut a shape and glue it to board or wood.

Craft knife
Board (wood), saw
Adhesive, spreader

Draw a design on it with sharpened chalk, and engrave the lines with lino cutters or X-acto gouges. Vary the width and the nature of the cuts.
Mix cellulose filler (with emulsion or powder paint if needed) and work it into the cuts with a spreader or flat knife. When it has dried off a little, wipe the surplus off the face of the block carefully with a flat-bunched cloth. The design should now show clearly.
If you want a stronger contrast, roll up the block with emulsion paint or oil based printing ink before you start with the cellulose filler (making sure you give it time to dry).
You can also use a one-colour linoleum cut (4). Make it into an inlay when you have finished printing with it.

Chalk
Linoleum cutters, X-acto gouges
Cellulose filler, spreader (knife)
Emulsion paint (powder paint)
Cloth

Inking plate, emulsion paint (oil based printing ink), roller
Old linoleum cut

4 Linoleum print

Use cork linoleum.
a Make a one-colour print:
Cut the linoleum to shape.
Draw a design on it with sharpened chalk or a light coloured crayon. This gives a similar effect to the final print when the cut-away lines show up lighter usually – unless you are printing with a light ink on dark paper.
Cut round these lines with a v-shaped cutter (No. 1 or

Craft knife
Chalk (crayon)

Linoleum cutters, X-acto gouges

Design for linocut. *left* Child
Linocut. *right* Child

2). Don't go too deep to start with. Continue working with these and other shaped cutters to develop further line and texture interest. Useful cutters at this stage are Nos. 3, 4 and 7, or other gouges. (See what each can do by using it in different ways.)
Ink and make a print (p. 175).
You may need to do more cutting after this first trial print. Continue cutting and printing until you have the effect you want.
Make further prints using different coloured ink or different coloured paper.

b Make a print with two or more colours.
Design and cut the block as in **a**, but cut lightly and don't cut too much away to start with.
Make several prints of this (p. 175), say six. It will be interesting to make each of these a different colour by changing the ink or the printing paper.
Clean the block and cut more away to develop the design further. This will print *on top* of the first prints; so what you cut away this time will leave the first colour showing. The rest will cover, or partly cover, the first printing.
Ink the block with a different colour. Lay it exactly over the first you made by lining up one edge and lowering it into place. Keep the block pressed to the paper and turn them over together so that the paper is on top. Press it out with a clean roller. Print this second cutting onto each of the first set of prints, again changing the ink colour for some of them if you want to.
You now have 6 two-coloured prints—all different colours.
If you wish to add more detail or colour, continue cutting, inking and printing in the same way.
This is called the 'waste' method of printing. You only use one piece of lino throughout, taking as many prints as you will need with the first printing. After that, you cut the block away more and more until very little is left.

Tools, as above, a

∨ ∨ ∪ ∪ ⊔

Lino cutter

c Make a print with two or more colours, using a different block for each colour.

Pin a right-angle of 1″ cardboard strip to a board.

Cut the linoleum to shape.

Draw a design on it, as in **a**.

Cut away all except the parts that are to be the first colour.

Cut printing paper 1″ larger all round than the block, and lay it on the right-angled cardboard strip, lining it up exactly with the outer edges. Pin it to one side of the angle. Later on, you will need to pin it back in exactly the same place for printing further colours; so note its position.

Fold back the paper.

Ink the block and lay it face-up tight into the angle. Lower the paper onto the block and press out with a clean roller.

Unpin the paper and lay it face-up on the table.

Take a second piece of linoleum the same shape as the first. Lay it exactly on the first *wet print*. Press them together, turn them over, and press out with a clean roller, so that the print transfers from the paper to the new block. This is now the guide for cutting the second block.

Cut away the printed areas and all other parts except those that are to be the second colour.

Ink the block with this colour and lay it in the angle as you did the first. Pin the paper back in its original position; lower it onto the block, and press out the print with a clean roller.

Unpin the paper. You now have two colours printed. Lay it face-up on the table and transfer its impression to a third block as you did before.

Continue to repeat this process for any further colours you may want. By printing these blocks in succession on the same piece of paper, you can make as many versions as you need of the multi-coloured block–each block printing its own contribution to the final effect.

d Make a *flat* linoleum mosaic or relief (1), (2).

(i) Make a roll-through print (p. 176).

(ii) Ink it and make a print (p. 175).

NB This may be an uneven surface. See p. 176.

Board, cardboard, craft knife, thumb tacks
See a, above
Tools as above, a

Printing paper

Inking plate, printing ink, roller

Two-colour linocut. Child

See above, 1, 2

Linocut. Student

5 Linoleum cut plaster cast

Design and cut a block as for a one-colour print (4). Or use an old one you have finished printing with.
Make a plaster cast (p. 174).
Colour the cast if needed (p. 174).
If the linoleum is inked before making the cast, the ink will pull off on the plaster in an interesting way.

See above, 4

6 Linoleum cut/mosaic/relief rubbing

When you make a suitable linoleum cut, mosaic or relief, make a rubbing of it (p. 179).

7 Linoleum–other uses

a Use it as an inking plate in print making.

b Use it as a table mixing palette for oil paints.

MACHINE PARTS

These include such things as parts of an old clock, radio, television, record player, typewriter, sewing machine, vacuum cleaner, food mixer, heater, mechanical toy, musical instrument, bicycle, car, machine workshop scrap.

1 Machine parts–study

Make a study of the shape and pattern of machine parts, using any suitable material or process.

2 Machine parts relief

Arrange a selection of machine parts to make a design. They can be metal, plastic or bakelite casing, rubber, and so on.
(i) Make a simple panel relief (p. 167).
(ii) Make a plaster bed relief (p. 168).

3 Machine parts impression and cast

Prepare a clay slab for making impressions (p. 163).
Press different parts of appliances into it to make a design. Lift each one out carefully afterwards.
(i) Biscuit/glaze fire the slab (p. 163) or
(ii) Make a plaster cast of it (p. 174).
Colour the cast if needed (p. 174).

4 Machine parts construction

Combine different machine parts to make a standing, hanging or projecting construction. It can be stationary or working, of course.

Fix the pieces by their own parts if possible, e.g. a spindle into a sleeve; by other metal parts that are suitable; by wiring them at neighbouring points; by cold or hot soldering or a recommended glue if the parts are light (clean all joining parts well, removing any grease or rust with white or mineral spirit, a dry cloth and emery paper).

Tin snips, wire, pliers, side-cutters
or
Cold solder, (solder with soldering iron)
or
Adhesive, spreader

White or mineral spirit, cloth, emery paper

5 Machine parts print

Use the different flat surfaces of machine parts.
Ink and print with them to make a design of their shapes (p. 175).

MAGAZINES

1 Magazine collage

Tear or cut magazine pages into various shapes.
Make a collage (p. 165), using the different tone areas of print, different thicknesses of type, and colour of illustrations. Superimpose pieces as freely as you need to get the effect you want.

Scissors

2 Magazine mosaic

Tear or cut up magazine pages into small, squarish shapes.
Make a simple panel mosaic (p. 167), using the different tone areas of print, different thicknesses of type, and colour of illustrations.

Scissors

3 Magazine relief

Cut magazine pages into strips of different widths, using both coloured and black and white parts.
Make them into spirals or curves by drawing them downwards between the thumb and a ruler edge.
Repeating this will tighten the spiral.
Arrange the spirals and curves into a design. They can be standing on their edge or on their side, and can be spaced, touching or interlocking.
Glue them to a suitably surfaced card. To stick a spiral on its edge, you may find it easier to glue an X on the

Scissors

Ruler (straight edge)

Cardboard
Paint, texturing material
Adhesive, spreader

card and lay the spiral on it, holding it at the tension you want until it sticks.

4 Magazine weaving

Cut magazine pages into strips of roughly the same width, but varying them a little. Use both coloured and black and white parts.	Scissors
Pin the ends of one set of strips (maybe the black and white ones) to a card, and weave the other strips (maybe the coloured ones) into them.	Pins, cardboard, craft knife
Unpin them. Trim and fold back the ends alternate ways, and secure with a touch of paste or gum.	Adhesive, spreader

5 Magazine print

a Tear or cut out paper shapes to combine into a design without too much overlapping.	Scissors
Glue them to a firm card.	Cardboard, craft knife
When quite dry:	Adhesive, spreader

(i) Make a roll-through print (p. 176).
(ii) Ink and make a print (p. 175).
This may only be possible a few times, as the paper pieces tend to come away after a certain amount of inking. A slightly stronger adhesive holds them longer.

b Twist magazine paper up tightly or loosely.
Press it into an inked pad and make a design of prints, using the accidental effects of the crumpled paper.

6 Magazine montage

Tear or cut out pictures from magazines and re-assemble them to make a new imaginative design.	Scissors
Paste these down to paper or cardboard.	Paper (cardboard), craft knife
You can get interesting results from cutting *through* pictures and using the different parts in an unusual relationship with each other.	Adhesive, spreader

MATCHBOXES

1 Matchbox design

On a sheet of paper, draw round a matchbox in different positions to make a design. Use the box flat, on its side, on its end, with its drawer pulled out to different lengths. Let the shapes overlap as much as you wish. Develop the design as a drawing, or as a painting, colouring the areas between lines.	Paper, drawing medium
	Paint

2 Matchbox collage

Cut down some boxes into parts.	
Arrange them as a flat design, using the various colours	Craft knife (scissors)

of paper and label, and the textures of the striking surface.
Make a collage (p. 165).

3 Matchbox mosaic

Cut up different coloured matchboxes into small squarish shapes.
Arrange them into a design, using the different colours of paper and label, and the textures of the striking surface.
Make a simple panel mosaic (p. 167).

Craft knife (scissors)

4 Matchbox relief

Arrange whole boxes (outers and inners, together or separately) to make a relief design. Stand them up any way; re-shape any you need to by cutting; use opened-out boxes for contrast.
Make a simple panel relief (p. 167).

Craft knife (scissors)

5 Matchbox construction

Use whole boxes (outers and inners, together or separately) to make a standing, hanging or projecting construction.
Assemble them, facing in different directions. Re-shape any you need to by cutting.
Glue them together one at a time.
Paint the finished construction if needed.

Craft knife (scissors)
Adhesive, spreader
Powder paint (emulsion paint)

6 Matchbox print

Make a design by printing with the different parts of a matchbox p. 175. Use the sides, the ends (with or without the drawer in), the edges, and the outer case squeezed into a new shape. In any one design you may only want to use one or two of these alternatives.

7 Matchbox–other uses

a As a bed for a small mosaic:
Mark round the box drawer on a piece of paper.
Arrange small objects or fragments into a design to fill the shape.

Drawing medium, paper
Beads, stones, shells, cheap jewellery, broken china, glass (*care here*), tile, metal parts

Make a mosaic in the drawer (p. 168).
Pins through the sides of the box into the plaster before it sets will hold the filling in.

Pins

b As a store for small items like beads, or for small amounts of material like sand.
You can build a nest of drawers of this kind by glueing several matchboxes together, with brass paper fasteners for handles.

Adhesive, spreader
Paper fasteners, bodkin,
(awl)

MATCHES

Use dead matches, or unused ones without the heads. Cut them down, shape them, and dip them in ink or paint if needed.

Craft knife
Ink (paint)

1 Match relief

a Arrange matches flat into a design.
(i) Make a simple panel relief (p. 167).
(ii) Make a plaster skimmed panel relief (p. 170).

b Make a relief, **a**. But fill in the spaces between matches with other materials.

See above, a
Matchbox material, sand-paper, coloured paper, texturing material, with adhesive

c Cut matches into various short lengths.
Sticking them flat and on end, and using the different heights to full effect
(i) Make a simple panel relief (p. 167).
(ii) Make a plaster skimmed panel relief (p. 170).
Paint or texture any areas you need to at the best stage.

Craft knife

Paint, texturing material with adhesive

2 Match construction

Glue a few matches together to start a free or a planned construction. Continue adding matches as each stage has stuck. Develop the construction in shallow depth, or to greater height. Watch the balance as it grows.
Paint or spray the result if needed.

Adhesive, spreader

Paint (spray)

3 Match relief–plaster cast

Make a relief (1a, i above).
Make a plaster cast of it (p. 174).
Colour the cast if needed (p. 174).

See above, 1a i

4 Match relief–rubbing

Make a relief (1a, i above).
Make a rubbing of it (p. 179).

See above, 1a i

5 Match print

a Make a relief (1a, i above).
(i) Make a roll-through print (p. 176).
(ii) Ink and make a print (p. 175).

See above, 1a i

b Cut and glue matches to a small wood block.

Wood block
Adhesive, spreader

Make a design of prints with it, using it in different positions (p. 175).

METAL SCRAP

1 Metal scrap study

Make a study of the shape, colour, pattern and texture of metal scrap, especially rusted, corroded or scarred pieces, using any suitable material or process.

Materials, tools as needed

2 Metal scrap relief

a Arrange a selection of metal scrap into a design and fix it to a suitably surfaced board.
Some ways of fixing:
Screw or nail through existing holes in the metal into the panel, or through holes made with a punch or drill.

Board (wood), saw

Screws, awl, screwdriver
Nails, hammer
Punch, hammer, (metal drill)
or

Pass fine wire round a few anchor points, and through a hole in the panel. Twist and secure behind.

Wire, pliers, wood drill
or
Solder, soldering iron (cold solder)
or
Adhesive, spreader
White or mineral spirit, cloth, emery paper

Solder them. Or glue them if the metal is light. Clean all joining parts well, removing any grease or rust with white or mineral spirit, a dry cloth, and emery paper.

Use their own parts.

b Staple chicken wire across a simple box frame.

Chicken wire, pliers
(side cutters), box frame, staples, hammer

Nail a board or wood back on.

Board (wood), saw, nails

Arrange a selection of metal scrap (including rusted pieces) into a design, and anchor them to the chicken wire with wire.
Lay it flat with the pieces upwards.
Mix plaster (p. 172) and pour it into the frame so that it rises to the metal. Shake it to find its own level. Colour from the rust will stain the plaster in interesting ways. Add further colour if needed (p. 173).

Wire

3 Metal scrap construction

Arrange and fit metal scrap together to make a standing, hanging or projecting construction.
Some ways of fixing:
Make use of their own parts: some may fit into others.

Wire them to each other at points that meet. Drill the metal if needed.

Wire, pliers, metal drill
or
Screws, awl, screwdriver, metal and wood drill, wood, saw, nails, hammer
or

Screw them to a wood support, concealed or not, depending on whether you want it to play a part in the final effect.

Solder them. Or glue them if the metal is light. Clean all joining parts well, removing any grease or rust with white or mineral spirit, a dry cloth, and emery paper.

The shapes of the metal scrap themselves may suggest how the construction could develop. Shape any parts you need to with the appropriate tools. Weight and balance the construction as you go along so that it stands firmly at all times and stages. Or plan the work from the start, making up the various parts separately maybe, to assemble all together.

Solder, soldering iron
(cold solder)
or
Adhesive, spreader
White or mineral spirit,
cloth, emery paper

Tin snips, hacksaw, pliers,
punch, hammer, metal drill

4 Metal scrap print

Use different flat surfaces of metal scrap.
Make sure they are clean. Ink and print with them
(p. 175) to make a design of their shapes.

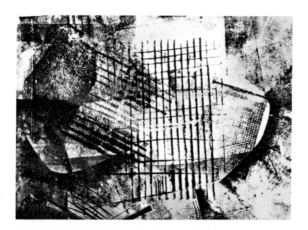

Metal scrap print. Child

NAILS

1 Nail relief

a Cut a shape of wood.
Plane or sandpaper the surface if needed.
Draw a design on it lightly with sharpened chalk or charcoal (you will be able to dust this off afterwards from between the nails).
Paint or texture any areas needed.

Wood, saw, plane, sandpaper
Chalk (charcoal), craft knife

Paint, texturing material with adhesive
Hammer

Select and drive in nails along the lines of the drawing, and to cluster or crowd in any areas needed. The effect will be determined by the size and height of the nails, the shape of the nail heads, the angle they are driven in at, and the spaces between them.
Paint the nail heads with a suitable paint if needed.

Emulsion paint (oil paint, metallic paint, powder paint)

b Prepare a wood panel as above, **a**
Draw a design on it lightly.
Drive in nails at salient points and stretch fine wire between them, winding it once or twice round each nail as you go. The effect will depend on the way the wires radiate, converge, cross, and rise or fall. Keep the tension throughout. It will help to put a touch of solder or glue where the wire goes round the nails—especially at the start, at joins, and at the end.

See above, a
See above, a
Hammer
Fine copper, tinned or brass wire, pliers, side cutters

Solder, soldering iron, (cold solder)
or
Adhesive, spreader

You can, of course, do both **a** and **b** directly without any pre-drawn design, letting the nails or wire determine how the work should develop.

c Cut a shape of board or wood.
Use flat (flooring) nails or oval nails—or round ones with the heads hammered flat. They can be new or

Board (wood), saw

Hammer

rusted, but clean the underside of rusted ones on
emery paper.   Emery paper

Arrange them flat to make a design, and glue them one   Adhesive, spreader
at a time to the panel.

You can paint or texture areas at any suitable stage.   Paint, texturing material
                                         with adhesive

2 Nail impression

a Cut a shape of board or wood.   Board (wood), saw

Draw a design lightly on it.   Soft pencil

Punch a dot pattern with a nail (or nails) along and   Hammer
between the lines in a close or open arrangement.

You can leave this as it is, or run a contrasting colour   Inking plate, printing ink,
of ink over the wood with a roller, leaving the pattern   roller
of impressions untouched.

b Prepare a clay slab for making impressions (p. 163).
Use any size of nail (or screw for contrast). Press the
heads into the clay to different depths, making a design
of the arrangement.

(i) Biscuit/glaze fire the slab (p. 163) or

(ii) Make a plaster cast of it (p. 174).

Colour the cast if needed (p. 174).

3 Nail print

a Use various nail heads. Paint them, or press them
into an inked pad, and print with them on paper
making a design from the arrangement of small shapes
(p. 175).

b Make a relief (1c). Keep it flat.

(i) Make a roll-through print (p. 176).

(ii) Ink and make a print (p. 175).

Be careful not to puncture the paper with the nails.

This may be an uneven surface. See p. 176.

c Make a nail impression (2a).

Ink and make a print (p. 175).

NEWSPAPER

1 Newspaper collage

Tear newspaper into pieces.
Use the different tones of the type and the photographs
to build up the areas of your design.
Make a collage (p. 165).

2 Newspaper modelling

a Twist or roll pieces of newspaper and tie them to   String (twine), scissors
form the rough shape of the form. Pack and tie in any
smaller pieces needed to fill it out. Make sure it will
stand if you want it to.

Soak some paper in paste, and wrap it round the form   Paste, bowl

Newspaper collage. Child

to complete the modelling, smoothing it into place.
Add as many layers as you need.

When the pasted paper has dried, paint it or cover it
with suitable materials, depending on the nature of the
model.

Powder paint (emulsion
paint), other materials with
adhesive

An alternative method of covering is to use strips of
butter muslin or cheese cloth soaked in delayed setting
plaster (see p. 173), emulsion paint, or cellulose filler.
Wrap them round the paper form in the same way, and
work in any further plaster or cellulose filler needed to
complete the modelling.

Butter muslin or cheesecloth
Plaster with size (emulsion
paint, cellulose filler)

This surface, when it dries, can be attractive in itself,
though you may wish to colour or cover it with further
materials.

Powder paint (emulsion
paint), other materials with
adhesive

b Make pulped papier mâché (p. 172).

For a simple form, use this as a broad modelling
medium as it is, or with some mixed plaster or cellulose
filler worked into it.

Plaster with size (cellulose
filler), bowl

For more complex forms, make a firm armature of
wood, wire or chicken wire first, and model the mixture
on it.

Wood, saw, nails, hammer
or Wire, pliers
or Chicken wire, pliers, side
cutters

When the model is dry, paint it or cover it with further
materials if needed.

Powder paint (emulsion
paint), other materials with
adhesive

NB This is a way to make puppet heads.

c Use an old picture frame with a simple right-angled
moulding if possible.

Picture frame

Cut a piece of board (hardboard or pegboard are suitable) and a piece of chicken wire a little smaller than
the outside measurements of the frame.

Board, saw
Chicken wire, pliers,
side cutters

Lay the frame face-down. Lay the chicken wire on it.
Lay the board on top of that. Nail through them both
to fix them to the frame.

Nails, hammer

Turn the frame over and pull at the chicken wire a
little to raise it in places from the board, tucking short

Bed for papier mâché relief

lengths of wood under the mesh to keep it raised. This
will help 'key' the papier mâché when you pack it in.
Mix pulped papier mâché (p. 172) with some mixed

Wood

Papier mâché relief

plaster or cellulose filler added. Press the mixture well into the frame, making it key with the chicken wire and the edge of the frame.	Builders' plaster (cellulose filler)
Model the surface like clay by adding and taking away. Texture or smooth it with any suitable tool.	Kitchen utensil, wood chip, piece of metal, trowel, spatula
You may prefer to draw a design for this first. Make your drawing on thin paper to the inside measurements of the frame.	Thin paper, drawing medium
Mix the papier mâché and pack it into the frame.	See above
Lay your design on it, smoothing it down a little to keep it in place. Prick through the outlines at close intervals. Remove the paper and join up the pricked dots in the mix with the same tool. Then model the surface as above.	Divider (compass)
When it is dry you can paint it if needed.	See above Powder paint (emulsion paint, oil paint—you need to size it for this, ink)
d Make a model in clay or plasticine; or carve a potato, turnip or similar vegetable.	Clay (plasticine, firm vegetable), craft knife
Cover it with layered papier mâché (p. 172).	
When the paper has dried, cut it round the middle with a sharp knife or hard-backed razor blade, take the model out, re-join the halves and stick them together with more strips of pasted paper.	Hard-backed razor blade
Paint or texture the finished form if needed.	Powder paint (emulsion paint), texturing material with adhesive

NB This is another way to make a puppet head.

NUT SHELLS

Some nuts you may like to use:
brazil, walnut, hazel, almond, coconut, chestnut.

1 Nut shell relief

Use half shells as far as possible, though include smaller pieces if needed. Do any further shaping with a craft knife or sandpaper block. You can fix the shells either	Craft knife, sandpaper

way up: be sure that any rounded surfaces are well anchored.

Arrange them into a design using just their own natural shapes, colours and textures. Or paint them. Or line their hollows with other materials.

Powder paint (emulsion paint)
Melted wax—candle, crayon, paraffin, cellulose filler—white or coloured, texturing material with adhesive

(i)   Make a simple panel relief (p. 167).
(ii) Make a plaster bed relief (p. 168).
(iii) Make a plaster skimmed panel relief (p. 170).

In (ii) and (iii) leave the shells a little proud of (above) the plaster, or make them level with it, depending on the effect you want.

2 Nut shell mosaic

Break up different shells into small, squarish pieces. Use their different colours and textures.

Hammer

(i) Make a simple panel mosaic (p. 167).
(ii) Make a plaster skimmed panel mosaic (p. 170).

3 Nut shell construction

Use a selection of broken shells. Do any further shaping with a craft knife or sandpaper block.

Assemble them to make a small standing form. Glue them to each other, or to a wood or cardboard support.

Paint the finished construction if needed.

Craft knife, sandpaper

Adhesive, spreader
Wood, saw (cardboard)
Powder paint (emulsion paint)

NYLON STOCKINGS

1 Nylon stocking appliqué

Cut up nylon stockings of the same or different shades and deniers.

Scissors

Arrange the pieces into a design using the effects of overlaying to create areas of varying tone and density.

Lay a piece of fabric flat, see p. 52. Transfer the nylon pieces in the order planned and sew them to it by catching them with short stitches.

Fabric, see p. 52
Thread, needle

Use related material with the stockings if needed.

(Net, organdie, silk, rayon, mesh, feathers, beads, buttons, other accessories)
Cardboard, craft knife
(board, saw)

Finish by stretching the supporting fabric over cardboard or board cut to size, and pulling it tight with long cross stitches behind.

2 Nylon stocking collage

Cut up nylon stockings of the same or different shades and deniers.	Scissors
Arrange the pieces into a design using the effects of overlaying to create areas of varying tone and density. Make a collage (p. 165) using a clear adhesive.	
Use related materials with the stockings if needed.	See above, 1

3 Nylon stocking modelling

Use a full-length or cut-down stocking. Pack it with any suitable soft material, pulling it in and tying it with thread at certain points to make a simple basic form which you can then elaborate on. Or you can do this by sewing if you prefer.	Scissors Other stockings, kapok, tissues, paper towels, soft fabric, cotton waste, cotton wool, foam plastic pieces, sawdust
Attach other materials needed to complete it by sewing, or by passing wire through the stocking, or by glueing.	Thread, needle Wire, pliers or
This is another way to make a puppet.	Adhesive, spreader

4 Nylon stockings – other uses

a Use a cut-down stocking as a strainer for any paint that has got bits in it (like dried film on oil paint). Stretch the nylon over a jar and fix it there with a good elastic band while you pour.	Jar (can), elastic band
b Use a cut-down stocking as a temporary 'mould' for plaster when you want to shape it by hand into an interesting form for carving. The plaster should just be starting to thicken when you pour it.	

PACKING STRAW

1 Packing straw collage

Cut a shape of cardboard or board.	Cardboard, craft knife
Separate strands of packing straw. You may need quite a lot.	(board, saw)
Glue part of the panel.	Adhesive, spreader
Press the strands flat onto it, close together or spaced, laying them in different directions. Continue adding strands to develop a design of the textures. Try to avoid getting glue on the top of the straw as it will probably dry shiny – and will make further handling difficult.	Scissors
You can vary the packing straw with other related materials, of course, and use texturing materials like sand in areas if needed.	(Wood shavings, string, twine, natural straw, texturing material with adhesive)

2 Packing straw model

Bunch and tie packing straw with string to make a shape.	String, scissors
Work wire through the straw to reinforce it or to thread further 'parcels' on to develop the shape.	Wire, pliers
Cover the straw shape by wrapping it with strips of newspaper or brown paper soaked in paste, or strips of butter muslin or cheesecloth soaked in delayed setting plaster, builders' plaster, cellulose filler or emulsion paint—or in any combination of these.	Newspaper (brown paper), paste, bowl or Butter muslin or cheesecloth, plaster with size (builders' plaster, cellulose filler, emulsion paint), bowl
Finish the form with paint or a texturing material if needed.	Powder paint (emulsion paint, ink), texturing material with adhesive

3 Packing straw print

a Make a straw collage (1).

(i) Make a roll-through print (p. 176).

(ii) Ink and make a print (p. 175).

See above, 1

b Lay a few loose strands on a board.

Make a roll-through print (p. 176). Move the strands or paper and make another print. Continue until you have made your design.

PAPER TOWELS

1 Paper towel dip-dye

Mix a dye and put it in a flat dish.

Dye, flat dish

Fold the paper towel lengthwise several times like a screen. Hold it, edge down, and just surface-dip it in the dye. Capillary action will draw the dye up into the paper a certain distance. Unfold the paper: the drawn-up colour shape will be repeated as a pattern.

In further experiements:

(i) Dip the paper as above, then fold it into a screen the other way and dip it again. This will make a different kind of pattern.

(ii) Fold it in other ways so that a different arrangement of edges touches the dye and draws it up into various designs.

Interesting effects come from using a second colour.

PERFORATED ZINC (Meat safe sheeting)

1 Zinc relief

Cut shapes from a sheet of perforated zinc.
Arrange them flat, curved or modelled to make a design.
(i) Make a simple panel relief (p. 167).
(ii) Make a plaster skimmed panel relief (p. 170).
You can use other materials with the zinc for contrast if needed.

Tin snips

(Opened-out can, metal gauze, metal foil, punched bar, wire, expanded metal)

2 Zinc 'window'

Cut two shapes of firm cardboard the same size.
Cut a design of corresponding windows in them.
Cut perforated zinc shapes a little larger than each window. Sandwich them between the cards and glue them there.
You can insert double zinc shapes in places with coloured acetate sheeting, gelatine or cellophane between them for different effect.
Set it up against the light.

Cardboard, craft knife

Tin snips
Adhesive, spreader

Acetate sheeting, gelatine, cellophane

3 Zinc sewing

Use any kind of threads that will go through the perforations of the zinc.
Sew the threads through the zinc in long or short stitches to make a design. Sew over or under previous stitches as often as you need to, building up different thicknesses of yarn, or getting greater variety of crossing colours and textures.
When you change or join yarns, knot them behind the zinc.

Twine, gift string, fine cord, embroidery wool and cotton
Scissors, needle

4 Zinc modelling

Cut shapes of zinc.
Bend or curve them to meet and make a form. Secure them to each other by threading fine wire through opposing holes and twisting it tight up to the zinc. Nip off the ends or tuck them in.
You can, of course, use other kinds of thin metal with the zinc, though you will need to pierce or drill them to take the wire for joining. Use a punch, nail or drill for this, depending on the metal.

Tin snips

Fine wire, e.g. florists' wire

(Opened-out tin can, metal foil, metal gauze, wire, punched bar, expanded metal)
Punch (nail), hammer (metal drill)

5 Zinc rubbing

Make a rubbing from a shape of zinc (p. 179).
Move the zinc (or the paper) and make another rubbing.
Continue in this way until you have a design of the perforated shapes.

6 Zinc print

Ink and make a print from a shape of zinc (p. 175).
Ink and print again on the same paper in a different position.
Continue in this way, over-printing earlier shapes if needed, until you have a design of the perforated shapes. Re-ink the zinc whenever you need to, using the same or different colours.

7 Zinc design

Lay a small piece of zinc on a sheet of paper.
Put two pencil points or ball-point pens through holes.
Hold them upright and work them in arcs against each other, moving them across the paper in different directions. Lift off from time to time to see how the pattern is developing.
Complete it as a design by itself or with other media.

Paper
Pencils (ball-point pens)

Other media

PLANTS

1 Plant study

Make a study of the shape, colour, pattern, texture and growth of plants, using any suitable material or process.

Materials, tools as needed

Tree study. Student

2 Plant collage/relief

Collect woody or husky parts of plants, and other dried plants:
rushes, heather, pampas grass, gourds, pine needles, cones, sea holly, ferns, honesty, seeds, pods, acorns, old

man's beard, thorns, seaweed, roots, tree bast, dry corn
on the cob, certain herbs, twigs.

Use the flatter specimens, or reduce to flatter shapes by
pressing or cutting. Trim any you need to. Combine
them into a design of shapes and surfaces.

Craft knife (scissors)

(i) Make a collage (p. 165) or a simple panel relief
(p. 167).

(ii) Make a plaster skimmed panel relief (p. 170) with
suitable plants.

You may find it easier to fix some plants by sewing or
wiring them if they do not glue well.

Thread, needle
or
Wire, pliers, awl

3 Plant mosaic

Collect woody or husky parts of plants, see above, 2.
Use them as they are if they are small and reasonably
flat. If not, break them down into smaller pieces.

Craft knife (scissors)

(i) Make a simple panel mosaic (p. 167).
(ii) Make a plaster skimmed panel mosaic (p. 170).

4 Plant modelling

Combine different woody, husky or dried plants, see
above, 2, to make a standing, hanging or projecting
form. Re-shape any that you need to by trimming,
paring, parting and so on.

Craft knife (pen knife,
scissors)

Fix the parts together with fine wire, thread, glue, or by
their own parts, whichever seems best.

Wire, pliers, side cutters,
bodkin
or
Thread, needle, bodkin, awl
or
Adhesive, spreader

Plant models. Child

If needed, make a simple, light framework of wood,
wire or cardboard for it first.

Wood, wire, cardboard
with tools for shaping and
fixing

5 Plant puppet

Combine different woody, husky or dried plants, see
above, 2, to make a puppet. It can be a rod, shadow,
string or glove puppet.

Use the shapes of the plants themselves as inspiration,
and re-shape them by cutting as little as possible. Join
them with fine wire, thread or glue, depending on the
plants you are using and the way you want the puppet
to work, e.g. a thread through a hollow stem, a small
cloth hinge.

Tools and materials
as above

Make a simple framework of more rigid materials if the
puppet needs support.

Wood, wire, cardboard
with tools

Construct any operating parts needed (this may have to be done early on) and attach the puppet.

Dowelling, thin bamboo, wire; carpet thread, wood cross pieces; glove fabric, other items and tools for fixing

You can also make a puppet from green plants if you use the ones that stand up for a while after being cut. Devise the best means of fixing and working them beforehand if possible. They will be short-lived anyway of course.

PLASTER

Pouring plaster

1 Plaster modelling

a Make a model by twisting wire or chicken wire together. Pack inside it with screwed paper or wire wool to fill out some of the space.
Staple it to a wood block if it needs support.

Wire, chicken wire, pliers, side cutters, paper (wire wool)
Wood block, staples, hammer

Mix plaster (p. 172).
Trickle it over the model so that it keys to the wire. As the plaster hardens, add more, until you have built up the shape. By controlled pouring and adding, you can bring the model almost to the shape you want, though further modelling and carving of the surface will probably be needed to complete it.

Kitchen knife, craft knife, piece of wood, metal, hard plastic, plaster rasp

You can build other materials into the model as you go along if needed. Key them well into the wire or plaster. Colour the finished model if needed (p. 173).

b Build a framework model with wire, chicken wire or wood, coming roughly to the shape you want.

Wire, chicken wire, pliers, side cutters
or
Wood, saw, chisel, mallet, nails/panel pins, hammer (Screws, awl, hand drill, screwdriver)

Fix it to a wood block or similar base if it needs support. Cut strips from an open-weave fabric.

Mix delayed setting plaster (p. 173).
Soak the fabric strips in it and bind them round the framework, filling it out to the shape you want by added thicknesses and by modelling on with more of the plaster-mix by itself.
Colour the finished model if needed (p. 173).

Plaster carving. Child

2 Plaster relief

a Staple or nail chicken wire to a panel of chipboard, blockboard or wood, forming it into relief shapes.

Alternatively, build up relief shapes from wood or metal scrap. Fix them to the panel by nailing, screwing or wiring.

Cut strips or shapes of any suitable open-weave fabric.

Mix delayed setting plaster (p. 173).
Soak the fabric in it and lay it over the relief shapes, pressing it down to get a hold. You can add more of the plaster mix by itself to complete the modelling if needed.
Colour the finished relief if needed (p. 173).

b Cut a board or wood panel.
Mix delayed setting plaster (p. 173).
Soak pieces of coarse fabric in it and arrange them freely on the panel, shaping and pressing them into a design of relief forms.

3 Plaster carving

Make a block of plaster by mixing it (p. 172) and pouring it into a disposable container and letting it set. You can give the plaster an interesting shape before it sets by squeezing and holding the container in that position for a few minutes. The plaster should be fairly quick setting. Such a shape is often an inspiration in itself and

Staples
Butter muslin or cheesecloth (scrim, coarse sacking, hessian or burlap), scissors

Plaster model on wood and wire. Child

Chipboard (blockboard, wood), saw
Chicken wire, pliers, side cutters
Wood, hand saw (metal scrap, hacksaw)
Tools, materials for fixing
Scissors (craft knife)
Butter muslin or cheesecloth (scrim, coarse sacking, hessian or burlap)

Board (wood), saw

Fabric, scissors (craft knife)

Sugar packet (similar food wrap, small polythene bag, small cardboard box, waxed milk container)

makes it easier to get away from the square block shape.
When the plaster has set, strip off the container.
Carve with any simple cutting tool and smooth it down
finally if needed with a plaster rasp or sandpaper.

Kitchen knife, craft knife,
penknife, chisel, (mallet),
hacksaw blade, coarse file,
large nail file, riffler,
plaster rasp, sandpaper

You can make an interesting change in the plaster by
adding sand or a similar material to it.

Sand or similar material
(see p. 166)

4 Plaster cast

a You can make a plaster cast of any reasonably simple
surface that you have carved in low relief or engraved
(p. 174).

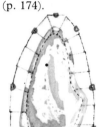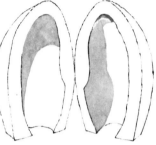

(1) Metal separators in place   (2) Plaster built up   (3) Mould halves separated   (4) Mould ready for pouring

b You can make a plaster cast of a model or carving
where you have used soft materials like clay, plasticine
or vegetables.
First make a mould: cut up some thin tin (opened-out
cans will do) into wedge shapes 1″ or so across.
Stand the model on a board.

Food can (thin metal),
tin snips
Board

Push the wedges into the model a little way to make a
continuous wall about 1″ high, dividing the model in
two. (For a more complicated model you would need
to divide it into three or more.)
Make a few small pellets of clay or plasticine and nip
them on to the outer edge of the 'wall' at intervals.

Clay (plasticine)

Now build a 1″ high wall of flattened clay or plasticine
round the base of the model 1″ or so from it, depending
on size.
Colour a little water with a blue bag or powder paint.
Mix the plaster (p. 172) to a thin cream, and add the
tinted water, stirring it in well.

Blue bag (powder paint),
jar

Pour or flick the plaster all over the model to an even
thickness about $\frac{1}{8}$″. Don't overlook any parts. Any
flooding should stop at the retaining wall you have set
up.
Mix some more plaster. Do not add tinted water.
Pour or flick this onto the tinted layer until the plaster
is about 1″ thick all over. Leave the top edge of the tin
strip showing—or expose it with a knife if it has got
covered, before the plaster sets hard.

Knife

When the plaster has set, turn it over and clear some
of the modelling material out from inside with a suitable tool.

Wire-ended modelling
tool (wire loop, spoon)

Stand the cleared mould upright on some sacking to
absorb any knocks it gets. Insert a small wood wedge
into the clay pellets you fixed round the tin strip and

Sacking
Wood wedge
Mallet

tap them lightly. Go from one to the other until the two halves of the mould begin to part along the dividing strip. If you hurry this stage, you may pull away parts of the inside of the mould.

With the halves separated, remove the tin strip and clear all remaining modelling material from inside the mould. Brush all over the inside with a little machine oil or liquid soap, going into all modelled details. This will prevent plaster sticking to plaster in the next step. Fit the two halves together and tie them tight with string. Plug any gaps round the join with clay or plasticine.

Mix plaster.

Pour some into the mould, turning the mould round as you do so to swill the plaster into all parts and lay an even deposit. Set the mould in a safe inverted position and add the rest of the plaster until the mould fills to the brim. Then leave it overnight, or longer.

Make sure the plaster is completely set (it should be quite cold). Stand the mould upright on sacking and chip away the plaster with a chisel and mallet, reducing it regularly all round. Hold the chisel between 45° and 90° for most of the cutting. Stop when you come to the tinted layer: you are almost at your cast model inside! Remove this final layer with care so that you don't snick the plaster underneath. Tap gently and try to 'spring' the plaster off.

Colour the finished cast if needed (p. 173).

An alternative way of making a mould: make your model as above.

Melt some paraffin wax in a tin can (stand the tin can in a pan of water over a low heat for this). Use a flat bristle brush and paint all over the model. Give it several coats, making sure you cover it completely each time. Clear some of the modelling material from inside. Warm a thin knife blade and cut round the wax, making two halves of the mould. Ease the halves apart. Clear out any remaining modelling material, re-join the halves and tie them together with string (it is rather brittle; take care). Fill in gaps with clay or plasticine. Support or cradle the mould.

Mix the plaster (p. 172) and pour it into the mould, turning it to lay a deposit. Pour the rest of the plaster in up to the brim and leave the filled mould standing inverted until the plaster has set.

Chip off the wax. It can be melted down and used again.

Note. A number of products are available nowadays for making flexible moulds (U.K.: Vinamold, U.S.: Liquid Latex). You can take several plaster casts from them. Afterwards you can melt the mould down and use the material again.

Machine oil (liquid soap), brush

String

Plaster cast. Child

Chisel

Cast from wax mould

Paraffin wax
Can, pan, brush

Knife

Clay (plasticine)

Jug

Chisel, mallet

5 Plaster engraving

Use a flat, smooth surface, not too big.
Lay it smooth side up on some scrap paper.

Glazed tile, piece of formica or hard plastic, metal plate, plate glass, ordinary glass (if it is safe to use) Scrap paper

Build a clay or cardboard wall round it 1″ or so high. Fix the cardboard with a staple or paper clip. Mix plaster (p. 172) and pour it in up to about 1″ deep. When it has set thoroughly, turn it over: the surface underneath should be smooth. Paint it evenly with ink, water colour or powder paint, and engrave a design through the colour with any pointed or sharp tool, exposing the white plaster.

Clay (cardboard, craft knife, stapler or paper clip)

Ink (water colour, powder paint)
Lino cutter, X-acto gouge, nail, nail file, divider, compass, bodkin, awl

6 Plaster print

Print from plaster. Student

Make a plaster block as above, 5.
Draw a design on the smooth side with ink and a fine brush.
Engrave the drawing with a suitable tool, as above, 5.
Give the plaster a light wash of size.
When dry, ink it and make a print (p. 175).

See above, 5
Ink, brush

See above, 5
Size, brush, bowl

7 Plaster – other uses

a As a bed for mosaic and relief work.
b As part of constructions with other materials.

PLASTIC DISPENSERS

These are mostly detergent or liquid soap dispensers, though there are many other kinds as well.

1 Dispenser relief

Paint several dispensers with emulsion paint or oil paint. Cut round them neatly so that you have tops and bottoms of varying depth, and some middles. Cut the middles into further rings, or cut them lengthwise into concave strips.
Make an arrangement of the different resulting shapes, using them either way up for the effect you want.
(i)   Make a simple panel relief (p. 167).
(ii) Make a plaster skimmed panel relief (p. 170).

Emulsion paint (oil paint)
Craft knife (scissors)

2 Dispenser construction

Use dispensers as they are, or cut up.
Assemble them to make a standing, hanging or projecting form. Fix them with glue, with fine wire, or by tacking them to prepared wood supports.

Craft knife (scissors)

Adhesive, spreader
or
Wire, pliers, side cutters, awl or
Wood, saw, nails, tacks, hammer

Paint the construction if needed.

Paint

3 Dispenser – other uses

a Use the end of a dispenser as a bed for a small mosaic.

b Use the end of a dispenser as a base for fixing a wire model in (or other similar models). Fill it with plaster and stand the model in it, supporting the model while the plaster sets.

Plaster

c Use the dispenser, with cap, for storing mixed paint or similar. The large kind, as used by hairdressers for bulk shampoos, are useful for storing liquid mixtures in quantities, e.g. pottery glazes.

PLASTICINE

1 Plasticine modelling

This is a traditional modelling material, available in several colours. It warms in the hands with use and becomes more supple. It shapes and joins easily, and does not set.
Make a model using the plasticine by itself or with other materials you can fix into it.

2 Plasticine print

Shape a ball of plasticine by pressing it on a board so that one face is flat.
Engrave or impress into this face with any simple tool or object.

Match, penknife, piece of hard scrap

Make a print (p. 175).
This surface will slowly lose its shape and details as you print, but it should stand up to making a fair size design. You could sharpen the detail with the tool again if needed, of course.

3 Plasticine impression and cast

Flatten a ball of plasticine. Make a design of impressions in it with suitable objects.

Small hard objects

Make a plaster cast of it (p. 174).
Colour the cast if needed (p. 174).

NB There are other similar modelling materials on the
market, e.g. Aloplast.

PLASTICS

Use the great variety of colour and modelled forms in
plastic.

1 Plastic mosaic

Cut or break up old plastic articles into small, squarish
shapes with a suitable tool. Use the flatter part of
articles like plates, saucers, toys, containers.
Make a simple panel mosaic (p. 167).

Craft knife, shears,
household scissors, tin
snips, hacksaw

2 Plastics relief

Cut or break up old plastic articles into different free
shapes with a suitable tool, as above, 1. Use from a wide
range of articles.
Make a simple panel relief (p. 167).

See above, 1

3 Plastics construction

Cut or break up old plastic articles into different free
shapes with a suitable tool, as above, 1.
Assemble the shapes to make a standing, hanging or
projecting form.
Fix them to each other with glue, or to a support of
wood with panel pins or finishing nails.

See above, 1

Adhesive, spreader
Wood, saw, hammer,
nails (panel pins or
finishing nails, tacks)

4 Plastics rubbing

Use a flat plastics mosaic or relief (1) (2).
Make a rubbing from it (p. 179).

See above, 1, 2

5 Plastics print

Use a flat plastics mosaic or relief (1) (2).
Ink it and make a print (p. 175).

See above, 1, 2

6 Plastics–other uses

a Use a plastic plate or saucer as a mixing palette for
paint.

b Use a plastic bowl for mixing things like plaster and emulsion paint–and a plastic jug for pouring them.

c Use a plastic container to keep things in, like small quantities of plaster, sand and small articles.

(Expanded) POLYSTYRENE (STYROFOAM)

You can get expanded polystyrene (U.S.: styrofoam) in the form of ceiling tiles, packing blocks, insulation panels, craft pieces, and in very thin wall insulation sheets.

You can cut it with a sharp knife, a heated wire, a heated needle (fixed in a cork), or a hot-wire tool specially designed for shaping polystyrene. You can model the forms and surfaces with any suitable shaped and heated metal instrument like a kitchen knife, a nail or metal scrap. Different tools leave different impressions. Direct heat melts it.

The crystalline whiteness of polystyrene is part of its attraction. It is worth protecting and using this quality. If you do want to colour it, use ink, dye, powder paint or emulsion paint. Do any drawing on it with a soft medium like brush and ink, or charcoal. Hard mediums will score it.

Craft knife (wire, needle and cork, hot-wire tool)

Kitchen knife (nail, metal scrap)

Ink (dye, powder paint, emulsion paint)
Brush (charcoal)

1 Polystyrene (Styrofoam) relief

a Cut out free or formal shapes from polystyrene. They can be spaced, touching, overlapping, or built up in layers.
(i) Make a simple panel relief (p. 167).
(ii) Make a plaster skimmed panel relief (p. 170).

Tools, see above

b Warm small, flattish metal shapes.

Metal scrap from electrical and mechanical appliances, metal cut to shape

Lay them on a polystyrene tile to make a design, letting them sink in a little. The softened edges of the polystyrene will hold them in place. If they do come out, glue them back again.
Colour the polystyrene if needed.

Adhesive, spreader
Colour, see above

2 Polystyrene (Styrofoam) mosaic

Cut up polystyrene blocks or tiles into small squarish shapes. Colour the tops of some of them.

Tools, see above
Colour, see above

Arrange the white and coloured squares or cubes into a design.
(i) Make a simple panel mosaic (p. 167).
(ii) Make a plaster skimmed panel mosaic (p. 170).

3 Polystyrene (Styrofoam) engraving

a Draw a design lightly on flat polystyrene. Use a heated nail or needle in a cork to engrave the lines. Make other texture impressions with a suitable metal tool or pieces. Roll printing ink or emulsion paint over the surface, leaving the engraved lines white.	Drawing medium, see above Nail (needle), cork See above, and 1 Inking plate, printing ink (emulsion paint), roller
b Drip hot wax (care here!) onto a flat polystyrene surface to make a design. You will get a different colour effect by rolling printing ink or emulsion paint over the surface before or after using the wax.	Candle wax (sealing wax, wax crayon) See above

4 Polystyrene (Styrofoam) carving/construction

Make a form to stand, hang or project.

a Draw a shape lightly on a polystyrene tile or block. Cut it out. You can use the shape itself or the shape it leaves. Fix the base into a block of polystyrene or wood if needed; or provide means for hanging or mounting it.	Drawing medium, see above Tools, see above Wood, saw
b Draw a shape lightly on a thick polystyrene block. Cut it out with a long heated wire that goes right through the block, or with a coping or pad saw. Continue carving the form, getting more rounded modelling with other suitable tools.	Wire (coping saw, pad saw) Tools, see above
c Carve a model, see above, **b**, but from several thicknesses of tiles. You can stick these together first or wire them temporarily during the cutting, and stick them afterwards.	Tools, see above Adhesive, spreader Wire, pliers
d Cut or carve polystyrene blocks and assemble them by glueing or wiring to make a multiple construction.	Tools, see above Adhesive, spreader, wire, pliers, side cutters
e Draw on a polystyrene block or tile an arrangement of shapes that you can cut away to make a pierced design. Mark the shapes to be cut out, and cut with a heated needle pushed right through, or with a fret saw. You can use coloured acetate sheeting, gelatine or glass to back or insert in the openings. Glue round the edges.	Drawing medium, see above Needle, cork (fret saw) Acetate sheeting (gelatine, glass) Craft knife (scissors, glass cutter) Adhesive, spreader
Stand or hang against the light. Colour or engrave the surface if needed. You could combine several pierced blocks to make a screen. Note. You can cast a polystyrene block in plaster (p. 174, 93) if it is suitable.	Colour, see above Nail

5 Polystyrene (Styrofoam) print

Draw and engrave a tile (3a).	See above, 3a
Ink and make a print (p. 175).	
You can print on fabric with this block. Lay a length of fabric on a table (pad under the fabric with a blanket or foam plastic sheeting).	Fabric Blanket (foam plastic)
Glue the polystyrene block to a block of 5- or 7-plywood.	Adhesive, spreader, plywood, saw
Roll generously with emulsion paint.	Inking plate (tray), roller, emulsion paint
Place the inked block face down on the fabric in the place you want to start your design, and hammer it with a mallet used handle down.	Mallet
Continue printing to build up your design.	

POTATO

1 Potato carving

Carve a potato into a simple form with a knife:	Pen knife (craft knife)
a Use the potato shape itself, particularly if it is unusual, and just carve enough to bring out what the shape suggests.	
b Carve a shape, leaving the peel, where appropriate, to give a contrast of colour and texture.	
c Carve freely into a potato, leaving no peel.	
d Carve parts that you can fit together as a larger model with wire or sticks. Use one or more potatoes. The parts can be fixed or moveable, depending on the model.	Wire, pliers, (matchstick, cocktail stick, oval nail)
Note. The carved potato will shrink and go bad. It can be preserved for a few days by immersing it in a 0·3 sucrose solution, but this is only a short term measure.	Sucrose solution
There are other ways of preserving the *shape* you have carved, though not the potato itself:	
Cover it with several layers of pasted tissue paper. When dry, cut the case in two, remove the potato and join the halves with more paper.	Tissue paper, paste, bowl, Craft knife (single-edged razor blade)
Or cover it with tissue paper as above, and let it dry. Cut a small hole in one end of the case, and stand it on its other end in a supporting container of some kind.	Tea cup (small bowl, box of sand)
Mix some plaster (p. 172).	Funnel
Pour it into the case slowly, using a funnel if needed, and making sure you don't trap an air bubble.	
When the plaster has set, remove the tissue case.	
Colour the plaster if needed (p. 173). If you have used coloured tissues, some of their colour will have stained the plaster—often attractively.	

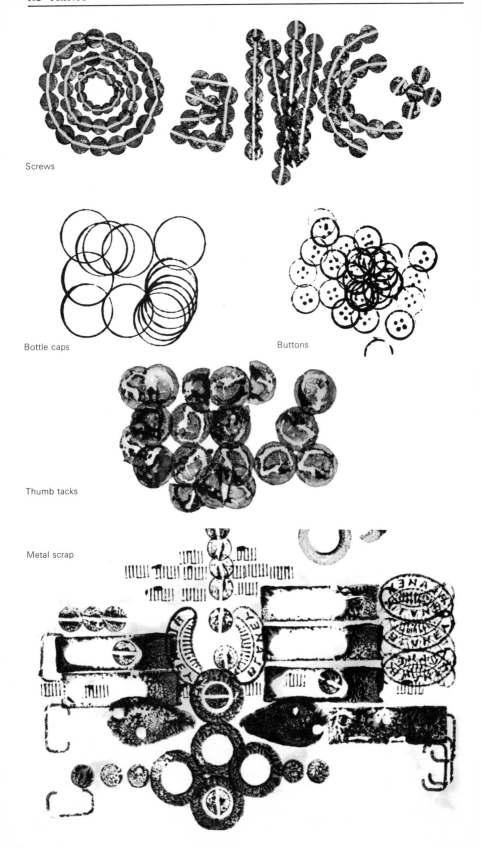

Screws

Bottle caps

Buttons

Thumb tacks

Metal scrap

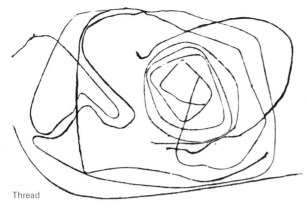

Thread

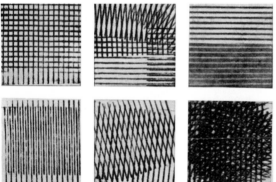

Rubber mat (roll through print)

Grass

Cotton reels (spools)

Twisted paper

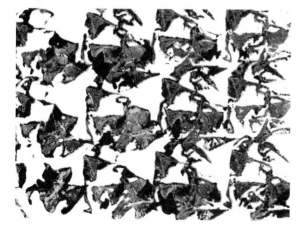

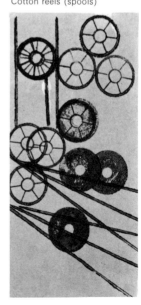

2 Potato modelling

a Using the potato as a centre, build into it with other materials to create a form. Sharp or pointed materials will go in easily: others will need a slot or hole made for entry. You will need the appropriate tools for these, of course.
Note. The model will only be as durable as the potato!

Thin metal, wood, hard plastic pieces, nails, wire, feathers, twigs, pins, some plants
Various tools

b Push wires through the potato from as many points as possible. Let them project a short way on either side. Run thinner wire from one to the other all round winding it once or twice round each projection. Fix each turn with a bead of solder or glue.

Rigid wire, pliers (side cutters)
Thin wire
Cold solder (solder and soldering iron), adhesive

As the potato dries out, pull it away, leaving the wire construction. Trim off any unwanted ends.

3 Potato cast

a Cut shapes from potatoes. Flatten one side a bit.
Make a design arrangement of them on a board, their flat side down.
Build a cardboard wall round them and seal it with clay or plasticine round the bottom edges.
Mix plaster (p. 172) and pour it over the potatoes until it has risen 1″ or so above them.
When the plaster has set thoroughly, turn the block over and remove the potato shapes with a knife. The surface will have an interest of its own, with the play of light over its hollows; but you may wish to colour it (p. 174).

Craft knife (kitchen knife)
Board

Cardboard, clay (plasticine)
Jug

b Cut one or more simple shapes from a potato, e.g. a cube.
Prepare a clay slab for making impressions (p. 163).
Press the potato shape(s) repeatedly into it to various depths to make a design.
(i) Biscuit/glaze fire it (p. 163) or
(ii) Make a plaster cast of it (p. 174).
Colour the cast if needed (p. 174).

,Craft knife (kitchen knife)

c Make a standing or stacked arrangement of potato pieces, e.g. chips, on a board.
Build a retaining wall round it with clay, 1″ away.
Mix plaster (p. 172) and pour it over the potatoes to about 1″ thickness, being careful not to disturb the pieces.
When the plaster has set, extract the pieces with a knife (easier when the potato has shrunk away).
Colour the cast if needed (p. 174).

Craft knife (kitchen knife), board
Clay

4 Potato print

a Cut a potato in two.
Ink the flat face and make a design of prints (p. 175). The shapes can be spaced, or touching, or overlapping: they can be in rows, or radiate from the centre or another part of the paper, or move in spirals and so on. Keep to one colour, or change colour.

Kitchen knife

Potato print. Child

b Cut a potato in two.
Make one or more V shaped cuts or gouged shapes in the flat face.
Ink it and make a design of prints as above, **a**.

Kitchen knife, penknife
(craft knife, lino gouge)

c Cut the end off a potato.
Ink it and print several times in any arrangement with the small exposed face, as above, **a**.
Cut off another slice.
Ink and print more shapes with this (larger) face.
Overprint wherever you want to.
Continue cutting slices off and printing with each new face exposed, getting larger towards the centre and smaller again towards the end.

Kitchen knife

d Cut and print with a potato as above, **c**, but make V-shaped or gouged shapes in the pieces.

Penknife (craft knife, lino gouge)

e Cut a small cube from a potato (it need not be a true cube) and print it repeatedly with different colours to make a mosaic design.

f Wind parcel string round a potato in spirals. Fix the string at intervals with pins.
Paint the string, and rock or roll the potato to make line prints.

Parcel string, scissors, pins, powder paint, paper

g Grate potato finely. Spread it out on a sheet of paper. Sprinkle dry powder colour over this. Lay another sheet of paper over this and press out under a rolling pin, or similar. The colour will transfer to both papers, but with different effects.

Grater, paper, dry powder colour
Rolling pin (jam jar, flat sided bottle)

RECORDS

Use unwanted records, whole or broken.
Break the older rigid records (78 speed) under sacking.
With care, you can cut them with a small tenon saw.

Tenon saw (scissors)

The newer flexible records will cut with ordinary household scissors.

If you want to drill them, use a metal drill.

Metal drill

1 Record mosaic

Use the older rigid records (78 speed). Soak the labels off and break or cut the records into small shapes.

Tools, as above

Use the different size and shape of the pieces and the different direction of the grooves.

Make a simple panel mosaic (p. 167).

Use other related materials with the records for contrast if needed. You may want further tools for cutting these, and other glues for sticking them.

(Flat plastic articles—kitchen ware, house fittings, old toys, old bakelite articles—radio cabinets, house fittings, formica)

Cutters, adhesive, spreader

2 Record relief

a Use the older rigid records (78 speed). Soak the labels off and break or cut the records into a variety of shapes and sizes.

Tools, as above

(i) Use them flat in one or more layers to make a simple panel relief (p. 167).

(ii) Use them at low opposing angles to make a plaster bed relief (p. 168).

In either case, use other related materials with the records for contrast if needed. You may want further tools for cutting or glueing these.

(See above)

b Be careful of fire and steam risk.

Heat and soften either kind of record. Do this in hot water or over steam in a large pan. While they are like this, you can shape them easily by hand and cut them with household scissors.

Large pan
Scissors

(i) Make a simple panel relief (p. 167).

(ii) Make a plaster bed relief (p. 168).

3 Record construction

a Use the older rigid records (78 speed). Soak the labels off. Break or cut the records into a variety of shapes and sizes.

Tools, as above

Assemble them as a standing, hanging or projecting form, fixing the pieces to each other if possible, or to a cardboard, board or wood support. Use glue, or drill and fix them with screws or wire.

Cardboard, craft knife
or
Board (wood), saw, panel pins (nails), hammer
Adhesive, spreader
or
Screws, awl, screwdriver, metal drill
or Wire, pliers, metal drill

b Be careful of fire and steam risk.

Heat and soften either kind of record as above, 2b. Combine the resulting shapes to make a standing, hanging or projecting form. Fix them as above, 3a.

See above, 3a

You can use melted pitch for further surface effects and bonding, and to fill in where needed. Melt in a tin can in a pan of water.

Pitch, can, pan

4 Record rubbing/print

From a flat mosaic (1) or a flat relief (2).
(i)   Make a rubbing (p. 179).
(ii) Make a roll-through print (p. 176).
(iii) Ink and make a print (p. 175).

5 Record plaster cast

From a flat mosaic (1) or a flat relief (2).
Make a plaster cast (p. 174).
Colour the cast if needed (p. 174).
Or use the plaster block to make further rubbings and prints as above, 4.

REELS, COTTON (SPOOLS)

Some thread reels are made of wood, some of plastic. They have their different qualities and effects.

1 Reel (spool) relief

Saw reels into horizontal, vertical or diagonal sections.
Paint the reels or panel—or both.
Make a simple panel relief (p. 167).

Small saw
Powder paint (emulsion paint)

2 Reel (spool) colour column

Paint stripes lengthwise on several reels. Wax or varnish the paint when it is dry if needed.
Lay them end to end, measure them and cut dowelling of the same length.
Bind the end of the dowel rod with insulating tape and fit it into one of the reels. Thread the others onto the rod in any order you prefer. Secure the last one in the same way as the first. (Using insulating tape rather than glue allows you to change the order of reels if you wish to get a different effect.)
Revolve the reels to make a column of changing pattern.
You may choose to make a very tall column and need to stand it in a heavier wood block. If you see the need for this, allow 1″ or so extra on the dowel rod to insert and glue in the block.

Powder paint (emulsion paint)
Wax polish (varnish)
Dowelling, saw
Insulating tape

Wood block, wood drill, adhesive, spreader

3 Reel (spool) impression

Cut away small parts from the reel.
Prepare a clay slab for making impressions (p. 163).
Make a design of reel impressions.
(i) Biscuit/glaze fire it (p. 163) or
(ii) Make a plaster cast of it (p. 174).
Colour the cast if needed (p. 174).

Craft knife (small saw, file, chisel)

4 Reel (spool) print

a Use the reel as it is, or cut away small parts of it.
Print a design (p. 175).
You may get a clearer print if you have a few sheets of
newspaper under the printing paper.

Craft knife (small saw, file, chisel)

Newspaper

b Ink the edges of the reel on a pad, with a brush, or
with a roller, and roll it in different ways on a sheet of
printing paper to make a design of lines.

Shallow container, piece
of foam plastic or felt, ink
or
Powder paint (ink)
or
Inking plate, printing ink,
roller
Printing paper

RUG CANVAS, ETC.

1 Rug canvas – weaving

Cut a shape of canvas.
Use any suitable thread or string for weaving and a
sewing bodkin or weaving needle.

Scissors
String, garden twine, gift
string, cord, knitting wool,
embroidery wool and
cotton
Sewing bodkin (weaving
needle)

a Weave a regular horizontal pattern into the canvas
mesh.

b Weave the threads in different directions to cross and
re-cross each other, building up a free design.

See above

2 Rug canvas rubbing

Use a small shape of canvas.
On the same piece of printing paper make a number of
overlapping rubbings, moving the canvas each time
under the paper to make a design (p. 179).

Scissors

3 Rug canvas print

Use a small piece of canvas.
(i) On the same piece of printing paper make a number
of overlapping roll-through prints (p. 176) moving the
canvas each time under the paper to make a design.
(ii) Ink and print the canvas (p. 175), making a number
of overlapping prints to form a design.

Scissors

SALT

1 Salt carving

Use a block of cooking salt or a salt block used by dairy farmers (unfortunately this is not as common as it used to be).
Carve it with any simple cutting tool.
Keep the shape simple. Its quality is in its coarse and sparkling white surface.
Keep the finished carving away from damp.

Craft knife (penknife, kitchen knife, sliver of wood, metal, hard plastic)

2 Salt cast

Carve a shape as above, 1.
Stand it on a board. Bend a cardboard wall round it, about 1″ from it and 1″ higher. Fix the wall with staples, clips or string, and seal round the bottom with clay or plasticine.
Mix plaster (p. 172). It must be quick setting!
Pour it round the carving up to the top of the wall.
When the plaster has set, remove the wall. Turn the mould upside down and run warm water onto the salt inside. It will dissolve, leaving its impression.
Brush the inside of the mould with machine oil or liquid soap. Support or cradle it.
Fill it with any suitable casting material.
Chip away the mould (p. 94).

See above, 1
Board, cardboard, craft knife (scissors), stapler (paper clips, string), clay (plasticine)

Jug

Machine oil (liquid soap)

Plaster (ciment fondu, U.S.: ready-made cement, pitch)

SAND

It is interesting, though not essential, to have different kinds of sand–different texture (coarse or fine), and different colours (white, yellow, brown, red, grey). You can make different colours by filling a tin can with sand and heating it over a ring for a while. The lower parts will heat more than the upper parts and will be darker usually. Separate the layers carefully.
In most of the following jobs you can also use other granular materials with the sand if needed.

Can

(Stone dust, slate dust, brick dust, building block dust, coal dust, coke dust, clinker dust, bird-cage grit, metal filings, glitter, rust dust, sawdust, chalk dust)

1 Sand drawing

Draw a design with glue on a piece of cardboard, squeezing the glue straight from the tube, or using a brush dipped in liquid glue.
Before it dries, cover it with sand.
When it has dried, shake the surplus off. You can paint areas in and around the drawing if you want added contrast. Or you can texture them with other materials.

Cardboard, craft knife
Adhesive (brush, glue pot)

(See above)

2 Sand relief

a Make a glued relief (p. 166).

b Draw a design on board or work directly without a pre-drawn design.

Build up the areas into different levels of relief with 'sculpted' paper, or with a modelling material:

If you use 'sculpted' paper, shape by scoring and bending, and glue it down well (by flaps if needed).

Drawing medium, board, saw

Paper, scissors, adhesive, spreader
or cellulose filler, (pulped papier mâché, plaster with size,

If you use a modelling material, make sure it has set well before going on to the next stage.

If you use expanded polystyrene, you can build up different thicknesses and glue and carve them as needed. Glue butter muslin or cheesecloth over the whole surface if needed to hold it all together, pressing it into all the relief forms.

Glue all, or parts, with sand (p. 166).

builders' plaster), bowl
or Expanded polystyrene or Styrofoam, craft knife (needle and cork), adhesive, spreader
Butter muslin, or cheesecloth, scissors, Scotch glue, brush, glue pot

3 Sand rubbing

Prepare a surface, see above, 1, 2a.

Make a rubbing (p. 179).

See above, 1, 2a

4 Sand print

Prepare a surface as above, 1, 2a.

(i) Make a roll-through print (p. 176).

(ii) Ink it and make a print (p. 175).

See above, 1, 2a

5 Sand–other uses

a Sand priming.

Cut a shape of board or wood for painting on, and prime it with emulsion paint (applied liberally) or with glue.

Board (wood), saw
Emulsion paint, broad brush
Scotch glue, brush, glue pot

Cover it with sand.

When dry, shake the surplus off. Paint all over again with emulsion paint. You can now paint on the textured surface with any medium.

b Sand box for carving.

Three-quarters fill a wooden box with sand. Use it to bed a block of stone, chalk or plaster for carving. The sand holds it steady and stops it turning as you carve. It also saves a lot of the dust which you can then just mix in with the sand.

Seed box (fruit box, old small drawer)

SAWDUST

Each wood gives its own coloured sawdust, and each saw gives its own kind of sawdust. Use a variety if you can get them.

1 Sawdust relief

a Make a glued relief (p. 166). Use other related materials if needed.

b Cut a shape of hardboard (masonite) or pegboard. Use it rough side up.
Strengthen it by nailing it to battens or wood strips if needed.
Mix sawdust and cellulose filler (or delayed setting plaster), and use it as a modelling material to build up a low relief on the board.
Leave or paint the finished relief as needed.

Hardboard (masonite, pegboard), saw
Battens or wood strips, nails, (panel pins), hammer
Cellulose filler (plaster with size), bowl
Powder paint (emulsion paint)

2 Sawdust modelling

Mix sawdust thoroughly with some weak glue or emulsion paint.
Put the mixture in a container that you can remove afterwards, and press it down well.

Scotch glue, glue pot (emulsion paint, bowl)
Cardboard box (sugar carton, polythene bag, waxed paper or plastic container)

When the mixture is set hard, remove the container. You should be able to carve the resulting block with simple tools.

Craft knife, penknife, file, chisel, small saw

3 Sawdust – other uses

Use sawdust for filling soft (fabric) models like puppets, toys and soft sculpture.

SCRAPS

1 Scraps design

a Draw round a selection of articles of any kind with any drawing or painting medium, letting the outlines touch and overlap in a variety of ways.
You can paint the spaces left between the lines to develop the design further.
b Use the shapes, surfaces and grouping of articles as a source of ideas for imaginative drawing and painting.

Drawing or painting medium, paper

See above

2 Scraps 'families'

Group articles into families according to their qualities or characteristics, e.g. shape, colour, surface, weight, transparency, hardness, flexibility, resonance, reflectiveness and so on.
See if any of the family groups suggest something to make. Discover by experiment the best way to fix them together.

Materials, tools as needed

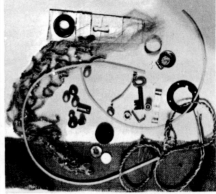

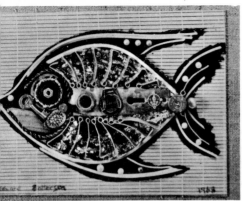

Scrap relief. Adult

Materials used in relief *left*

Scrap model

Scrap appliqué. Student

3 Scraps—other uses

Use articles of general scrap in different combinations
to make:
a A collage (p. 165).

b An appliqué or embroidery.

Thread, needle, scissors,
fabric support

c A mosaic (p. 167, 168).

d A relief (p. 167, 168).

e A carving.

Tools. See under Stone,
Wood and other sections

f A model.

Various tools

g A construction.

Various tools

h An impression (p. 163).

i A plaster cast (p. 93, 174).

j A rubbing (p. 179).

k A print (p. 175).

l Improvised tools for other activities.

Various tools

SEEDS

1 Seed mosaic

Set out as many different kinds of seed as you can in separate piles or boxes. Use other related materials with them if needed:

maize, sunflower seed, millet, (some pet foods, e.g. parrot, hamster, contain a variety), lentils, split peas, pearl barley, rice, peppers, certain cereals.

Cut a shape of cardboard or board.

Draw a design lightly on the board and select the seeds you need for it.

Make a simple panel mosaic (p. 167).

Stick the seeds into place by glueing small areas of the board at a time and transferring the seeds to them. Don't make the seeds too wet or they will swell and come away.

Cardboard, craft knife
(board, saw)
Drawing medium

SHAVINGS

Different woods give different coloured shavings, and different settings of planes give different kinds. Use a variety if you can.

1 Shavings collage

Use the shavings flat (and trimmed if needed), or use their natural springy curves and spirals as part of your design.

Make a collage (p. 165).

You can stick them down on edge as well, of course, making a higher relief effect (hold them down in the tension you want them until you are sure they have stuck and won't 'unwind').

You may like to use other related materials as well.

(Sawdust, wood chips, knots that have come away, turnings from a brace and bit)

2 Shavings – other uses

The decorative curls and spirals of many shavings make them useful for work with puppets and other kinds of modelling.

SHELLS

1 Shell study

Make a study of the shape, colour, pattern and texture
of a shell, using any suitable material or process.

Materials, tools as needed

2 Shell relief

Use whole, half, or broken shells:
crab, lobster, oyster, mussel, limpet, whelk, winkle,
razor, sea urchin, tropical shells, snail, tortoise, egg.
Use them either way up depending on the colours and
textures you want.
(i)   Make a simple panel relief (p. 167).
(ii) Make a plaster bed relief (p. 168).

3 Shell mosaic

Break up an assortment of shells into small shapes.
(i)   Make a simple panel mosaic (p. 167).
(ii) Make a plaster bed mosaic (p. 168).

Hammer

4 Shell construction

Use a selection of broken shells.
Assemble them to make a small standing form. Glue
them to each other, or to a cardboard or wood support.

Adhesive, spreader
or
Cardboard, craft knife
(wood, saw, panel pins
or finishing nails, hammer)

5 Shell impression and cast

Prepare a clay slab for making impressions (p. 163).
Use clearly marked (ridged) shells, and press them into
the clay to make a design of their shapes and textures.
Lift each one off cleanly afterwards.
(i)   Biscuit/glaze fire the slab (p. 163) or
(ii) Make a plaster cast of it (p. 174).
Colour the cast if needed (p. 174).

SILVERPAPER, METAL FOIL

1 Silverpaper and foil mosaic

Cut up silverpaper and other metal foils into small
squarish shapes. You may wish to use other kinds of
paper with them for contrast.
Make a simple panel mosaic (p. 167).

Scissors
(Other papers)

2 Silverpaper and foil collage

Cut up silverpaper and foil into different shapes.   Scissors
Make a collage (p. 165).

3 Silverpaper and foil engraving

Use a full sheet of silverpaper or metal foil.
Paste several layers of newspaper together to make a pad   Newspaper, paste, brush,
a little smaller than your silverpaper or foil.   bowl
Lay the silverpaper on this pad, smooth it out, and turn
it under round the edges.
Engrave a design on it by pressing with a slightly   Knitting needle (old ball-
blunted point, being careful not to go through the   point pen, match, shaped
silverpaper. The impressed design will remain fixed as   piece of wood)
the pasted paper dries.
With care, you can take a rubbing or a print of this
when it is really hard (p. 179, 175).

4 Silverpaper and foil relief

Foil relief

Build up layers of cardboard and glue them to a board   Board, saw
to make a relief design. Pare and shape any edges needed   Cardboard, craft knife
to 'model' the relief forms more roundly.   Adhesive, spreader
Parts of plastic doilies and tablecloths and similar
embossed materials can be glued on for special decora-   (Embossed materials)
tive effect.
Glue silver or other metal foil sheets over it, pressing   Scissors
them down well into all the surface modelling. You can
engrave further patterns or textures by pressing with a   (Engraving tool, see
slightly blunted tool into the foil.   above, 3)

5 Silverpaper modelling

Press out a flat sheet of silverpaper or foil.
Fold, twist and shape it into a form with the fingers or   Fountain pen cap,
with simple tools.   nail file, match

6 Silver foil casting

Crumple the thicker kind of silver foil into deep
undulations. Lay it down.
Mix plaster (p. 172) and pour it in, filling all the depressions to the top.
When the plaster has set, remove the foil. The small
plaster shapes that come away may be interesting in
themselves or suggest further slight shaping with a knife   Craft knife, nail file
or file.
Colour them if needed (p. 173).
The different pieces may fit together well for mounting
as a plaster skimmed relief (p. 170).

SLATE

You can use slate in its natural chunky or flaked form as
it is found on hill sites and rock quarries, or you can use
slates trimmed ready for roofing. Broken or split ones
can sometimes be had for the asking from a builder.
There are a number of ways you can trim slate to the
shape you want it:
Saw it.   Handsaw (tenon saw,
                                                              hacksaw)
Score it along a line with a pointed tool or a flat saw cut; Spike, wood block,
lay it on a block of wood with the unwanted part over-   hammer
hanging, and tap this part along the line until it comes
away.
'Bite' at the edges with pliers, reducing it a little at a   Pliers
time.
Use a stone chisel or claw (careful of splitting here).   Stone chisel (claw),
                                                              mallet
If you need to pierce slate, use a metal drill or gently   Metal drill
hammer a nail or metal spike through it.   Nail (spike), hammer

1 Slate relief

Select pieces of natural or trimmed slate. Trim them   Tools, see above
further if needed.
Arrange them spaced or touching, or let them 'ride'
each other, making sure that large overhanging parts
have some support from the slates underneath.
Make a simple panel relief (p. 167).

2 Slate mosaic

Break or cut up different coloured slates into small   Tools, see above
pieces.
(i) Make a simple panel mosaic (p. 167).
(ii) Make a plaster bed mosaic (p. 168).

3 Slate engraving

Use a smooth faced piece of slate which is not flaking.   Tools, see above
Trim it to the shape you want.

Draw a design on it with sharpened chalk.	Chalk, craft knife
Engrave along the lines with a cutter or pointed tool.	V-shaped X-acto tool,
Deepen the lines, and texture or pare away any areas	stone carving point or
you need to, using any suitable tool.	gouge, metal spike, awl,
You can mount the finished engraving as it is (it will'	large nail, claw
have subtle contrasts of surface); or you can rub over	
lightly with wax or oil to bring out the contrasts. Fix it	Wax (oil), cloth
to a suitably surfaced board or wood panel with glue, or	Board (wood), saw
by drilling and fastening with screws.	Adhesive, spreader
	or
	Metal drill, screws, awl,

4 Slate carving

screwdriver

Shape a piece of chunky or flat slate with any suitable	Tools, see above
tools, letting the natural forms or outline of the slate	
give you a start and suggest how the carving should go.	
You can leave the finished shape in its tooled state, or	
smooth it further with emery paper.	Emery paper
Wax or oil will bring out its deeper colours.	Wax (oil), cloth

5 Slate construction

Trim chunky or flat slate with any suitable tools.	Tools, see above
Assemble the pieces to make a standing form.	
Fix them together with glue or cement (1 cement:3	Adhesive, spreader
sand). Add slate dust if needed to tone it in. Arrange to	or
support the slate while it is setting.	Cement, sand, bowl
	(shovel, board)

6 Slate rubbing/print

Make an engraved slate (3).	See above, 3
(i) Make a rubbing (p. 179).	
(ii) Ink it and make a print (p. 175).	
Lift the paper carefully after printing: you may have to	
lay it back and press it out again if it is too faint.	

SOAP

1 Soap carving

a Use any kind of bar or tablet soap, though some carve	
better than others.	
Carve it in the hands with a pen knife or craft knife to	Penknife (craft knife)
make a simple form. Pare a little away at a time.	

b Use a transparent soap, like Pears.	
Carve it in the hands with a pen knife or craft knife.	Penknife (craft knife)
Hold it up against the light from time to time to see the	
effect of the different levels of cutting. You can discover	
various depths of colour and luminosity, and develop	
your carved form to exploit these qualities.	

To mount it effectively, cut corresponding holes the same shape as the soap in two pieces of (dark) cardboard. Fix them together about $\frac{1}{2}''$ apart by glueing small wood blocks (or similar) between them. Insert the finished soap carving. A thick elastic band round the soap, front and back, will keep it in place.
Set it up against the light.

Cardboard

Adhesive, spreader, wood blocks
Elastic bands

SPILLS (WOOD SPLINTERS)

Use plain cedar wood spills or dyed ones.
Arrange them tight up together, spaced out, overlapping, built up, whole or cut down.

1 Spill (splinter) relief

Arrange the spills flat or on edge, making a design of their directions and using any differences of length, width or colour. If you are using dyed spills, you may want to limit the number of colours.
(i) Make a simple panel relief (p. 167).
(ii) Make a plaster skimmed panel relief (p. 170).

Craft knife

2 Spill (splinter) construction

Assemble and glue spills together to make a standing, hanging or projecting form. Cut or trim any you need to as you go along, and make sure each part has stuck before going on to the next.

Adhesive, spreader
Craft knife

3 Spill (splinter) rubbing/print

Make a relief (1), using the spills *flat*.
(i) Make a rubbing (p. 179).
(ii) Make a roll-through print (p. 176).
(iii) Ink and make a print (p. 175).

See above, 1

4 Spill plaster cast

Make a relief (1), using the spills *flat*.
Make a plaster cast of it (p. 174).
Colour the cast if needed (p. 174).

See above, 1

STONE

Stone carving

Stone carving. Child

Use any reasonably soft stone to start with, like sandstone or limestone, just to get the feel of the different kinds of tools and mallet. You may like to try harder stones like granite and alabaster later. All stone has its own distinctive character, composition and texture, and these will play an important part in how you carve them.

a Carving in the round.
If your stone is a good size and fairly heavy, just stand it on sacking on a stout bench. If it is smaller and lighter, stand it in a wooden box of sand on the bench to stop it moving too much.

Sacking (wooden box, sand)

Use a few simple mallet head tools, say: $\frac{1}{4}''$ chisel, $\frac{1}{2}''$ shallow gouge, $\frac{3}{8}''$ deeper gouge, a medium point, $\frac{1}{2}''$ claw (you will find it useful to get a claw-bit holder; you can then insert a claw bit and renew it whenever needed without replacing the whole tool). Enlarge the range of these tools by adding more shapes and sizes as you can. A further useful reducing tool to have is a Bouchard hammer which has points on its striking surface to reduce the stone evenly by hammer action. You also need an iron dummy mallet, say $1\frac{1}{2}$ lbs. in weight.

Tools, see opposite

Carve directly into the stone (the point is useful for much of the work), discovering forms and surface textures as you go along.

Or sketch on paper the shape you want to carve from the stone; then sketch the shape on both sides of the block. Mark with an X the high points that you will want to keep, and carve away from these to the deeper levels with the tools that feel right for the job. Use them at the angle you find best. Work confidently, but watching out for any tendency in the stone to split. Go cautiously as you approach the shape you are working towards. You can finish off with a stone rasp or rifflers to smooth down smaller areas. The tool marks are often best left as part of the final surface.

Stone carving tools

Stone rasp, riffler

If you use harder stone you will want hammer head tools and an iron lump hammer about 2 lbs. in weight. Sharpening tools (really a specialist's job) is done on a carborundum grinding wheel or a carborundum rubbing stone.

b Carving in relief.
Lay the block flat on some folded sacking on the bench.
Work with any of the tools mentioned above, **a**.
Carve directly into the stone, discovering relief forms
and surface textures as you go along.
Or sketch on paper the design you want to carve; then
sketch it out on the face of the stone, marking the high
points with an X. Carve from these down to the deeper
levels in carefully controlled stages, watching how light
and shadow affect the definition at different levels. Keep
the stone turned to the best position for cutting.
Keep your tools sharp at all times.

Sacking
Tools, see above, a

Drawing medium, paper

STONES

Use stones found on the land, in rivers, or by the sea.
There is, of course, an almost endless variety to choose
from, in shape, size, colour and texture.

1 Stone study

Make a study of the shape, colour and texture of stones,
using any suitable material or process.

Materials, tools as needed

2 Stone relief

a Arrange different stones into a design, using any
shape, colour or texture that is appropriate.
Make a plaster bed relief (p. 168).

b Arrange *flat* stones of different colour and texture
into a design.
(i) Make a simple panel relief (p. 167).
(ii) Make a plaster skimmed panel relief (p. 170).

c Arrange different shaped stones to fit as a design on a
wood, chipboard or blockboard panel.
Build up the areas of the design with layered shapes of
polystyrene (styrofoam) or soft insulation board. Shape
these raised areas by further cutting, and paint or
texture them if needed.

Wood (chipboard,
blockboard), saw
Polystyrene or Styrofoam,
craft knife (needle, cork),
adhesive, spreader
or
Insulation board or
celotex, saw, surform,
sandpaper, adhesive,
spreader
Powder paint (emulsion
paint), texturing material
with adhesive
Wood gouge (X-acto
gouge), adhesive, spreader

Cut away hollows to bed the stones, and glue them into
place.

Stone mosaic. Adult

3 Stone mosaic

Arrange small squarish stones into a design using their different colours and textures.
(i) Make a simple panel mosaic (p. 167).
(ii) Make a plaster bed mosaic (p. 168).

4 Stone painting

Use the different surfaces of a stone to paint on. Either paint to bring out some form in the stone itself, or decorate with pattern in keeping with it.

Any paint

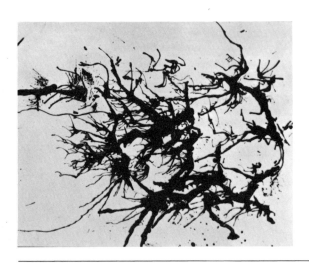

Ink-blown design. Child

STRAWS

Use natural straws or manufactured ones (milk straws) depending on the job you are doing.

1 Straw 'ink blown' design

Spill a few blots of ink on a sheet of paper and blow them through a milk straw. The ink will fan and spread to make different shapes which you can control by the direction and angle of blowing.

Ink, paper

2 Straw collage

Cut straws to different lengths.
Use them straight or bent, spaced or close up together,
to make a design.
Make a collage (p. 165).

Scissors (craft knife)

3 Straw construction

Cut straws to different lengths.
a Thread them together to make an open construction
of radiating and converging lines, using needle and
thread, or fine wire. You can make balanced geometric
shapes or freely assembled ones. They can stand, hang
or project.

Scissors (craft knife)

Thread, needle (fine wire,
pliers or side cutters)

b Build up straws into a construction by glueing them
parallel or at various angles to each other. Trim them as
you go along.

Adhesive, spreader,
Scissors (craft knife)

4 Straw rubbing/print

Make a flat collage of natural straws (2)
(i)   Make a rubbing (p. 179).
(ii) Make a roll-through print (p. 176).
(iii) Ink and make a print (p. 175).

See above, 2

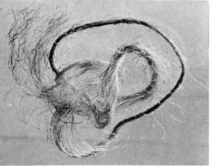

STRING

All kinds of string will have a use somewhere, but you
will want to use the right kind for the job you are doing.

1 String collage/relief

a Soak the string in paste, gum, rubber cement, warm
glue or emulsion paint, and flake it freely into a design
onto a piece of cardboard or board cut to shape. Press
it down along all its length to make sure it sticks.

Adhesive (emulsion
paint)
Cardboard, craft knife
(board, saw)

The panel itself can be coloured or textured beforehand or afterwards.

b Cut a shape of cardboard or board.
Draw a design lightly on it (just general outlines). Use lengths of different coloured string (you can make these yourself by dipping white string into ink or dye).
Glue one area at a time and flake or coil the string down on it to follow and fill out the drawn design. Trim the string as you go along. Control the development of the design by the directions and colours of the string, using its continuous flowing quality wherever possible. Introduce other textures if you need to.
You could, of course, do the collage directly without a pre-drawn design.

Powder paint (emulsion paint) texturing material with adhesive
Cardboard, craft knife (board, saw), drawing medium
Ink (dye)
Adhesive, spreader
Scissors

(Other texture)

c Cut a shape of chipboard, blockboard or wood.

Chipboard (blockboard, wood), saw

Draw a design on it lightly.
Drive in panel pins or finishing nails at intervals along the lines.

Pencil (charcoal)
Panel pins or finishing nails, hammer

Paint or texture any areas you need to.
Soak the string. Stretch it between the panel pins to create a design of tensions. The lines can converge, radiate, cross and run parallel. It will normally be enough just to turn the string once round a pin, though occasionally you may need to knot it. A bead of glue will secure it either way.
You could, of course, work directly without a pre-drawn design.

Paint, texturing material with adhesive

Glue

2 String weaving

a Cut several lengths of string, about 3' to 4'. Tie them to a rod close together, and rest the rod so that the strings hang.
Tie a small weight to the bottom of each string. This is now a hanging loom, with each string a warp.
Wind a different kind of string round a small shaped piece of wood (you could whittle it yourself) to serve as a shuttle. Start at the bottom, tying it to the first warp, then continue to weave it, working across and upwards to make a pattern. Change the string to vary the effect whenever needed. Keep the warp strings vertical throughout (don't pull too tight). Finish off with a knot.
Undo the weights and tie the strings back over the bottom weft, trimming off any ends. Undo the strings from the rod and tie them back over the top weft, trimming off the ends.

Scissors
Dowelling

Nut (bolt, pebble, small metal scrap, clothes' peg, clothes pin)

Shuttle

b Wind string round a stout card to make a simple warp. It helps to notch the card at the top and bottom first. Use a weaving needle or a sewing bodkin.
Weave different kinds of string into it to make a pattern. When the weave is complete, cut across the unwoven side and secure by knotting the warp ends to each other in pairs. Trim the ends.

Cardboard
Craft knife (scissors)
Weaving needle (sewing bodkin)

String embroidery. Student

3 String embroidery

Stretch a piece of fabric over a board or frame by staples or long cross stitches at the back. The colour and texture of the fabric should be right for the string you will be using.

Fabric, board (frame), staple gun

Arrange different kinds of string into a design on the fabric, and catch them into place with small stitches. Or sew with different stitches using fine string and thread.

Thread, needle

Use other threads or fabric pieces for further effect.

Other thread, fabric

4 String rubbing

Make a collage (1a, b).
Make a rubbing of it (p. 179).

See above, 1a b

5 String print

a Make a collage (1a, b).
(i) Make a roll-through print (p. 176).
(ii) Ink and make a print (p. 175).

See above, 1a, b

b Glue string round a drum.

Jar (bottle, cotton reel or spool, round tin can)
Adhesive, spreader

Paint or ink the string, and print with it by rolling it in different directions across the printing paper. Re-ink whenever needed.

Powder paint (emulsion paint, ink), printing paper

6 String elevation modelling

a Soak the string in glue or emulsion paint.
Twist and turn it into a small shape. Support the shape while it is drying. When dry, it will be fairly rigid.

Scotch glue, glue pot (emulsion paint, bowl)

b Soak the string in glue.
Lay it down in a design on a flat sheet of transparent or semi-transparent paper. Try to avoid dragging any glue across the paper.

Scotch glue, glue pot
Greaseproof paper (strong tissue paper, imitation Japanese paper, cellophane, other thin printing paper)

When dry, the string will have formed quite a rigid tracery on the paper. Stick into the 'window' shapes any further transparent coloured papers you may need for effect. Use a clear adhesive.

Trim off the paper round the string and stand or hang it against the light.

Scissors

Cellulose paste
U.S.: Acrylic

7 String drawing

Use fine twine. Soak it in ink and lay it on a sheet of paper. Lay another sheet of paper over the first, and holding it down flat under a board, draw the string out towards you with different movements from between the 'sandwich' of paper. There will be a line and tone 'drawing' on both pieces of paper. With experience, you can control the effects more.

You can add to the design of marks by re-inking the twine and repeating the process.

Ink, paper

8 String–other uses

Use string as it is, or teased out into fine or fluffy strands, as a textural material in other work.

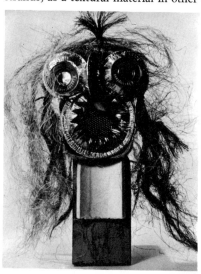

SUGAR (CONSTRUCTION) PAPER, PASTEL PAPER

There are many different colours or sugar or construction paper and pastel paper. Make full use of the range if you can. (Some of the colours do tend to fade after a time in the light.)

1 Sugar (construction) paper collage

Tear or cut sugar paper into different shapes. Use scraps and off-cuts, and the backs of old drawings or paintings. (It is worth saving these if they are in reasonable condition.)

Make a collage (p. 165).

Scissors

Sugar paper collage. Child   Sugar paper collage. Child

2 Sugar (construction) paper mosaic

Use as many of the different coloured papers as you
need. Tear or cut them into small, squarish shapes.   Scissors
Make a simple panel mosaic (p. 167).

3 Sugar (construction) paper–other uses

a As a good drawing and painting paper, especially for
bold, free work. Its texture makes it pleasant to work on
with most broad media like charcoal and powder paint.

b As a good general paper for mounting light collages,
mosaics and graphic work.

THREAD

1 Curve stitching

Use a piece of card or thick paper, and a contrasting   Card (paper)
coloured thread.   Craft knife (scissors)

Draw a simple geometric shape on the card (square,   Pencil
rectangle, diamond, oval, circle). Mark equally spaced
dots round it.   Needle

Prick through each dot with a needle.

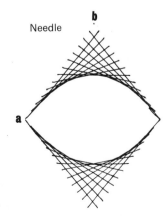

Thread the needle and knot the thread.
(i) With an angled shape, start from behind the card;
sew from corner hole A to the next corner along B;
come up through the hole in advance of B and return to
the hole in advance of A; continue in this way until you
return to the first hole; finish off under the card with a
through stitch and knot–or with a bead of glue.
(ii) With a curved shape, start from behind the card;
sew up from any point to the next quarter-point away,
e.g. from 12 o'clock to 3 o'clock; come up through the
hole in advance of this, and return to the hole in advance

of the first point; continue in this way until you return to the first hole; finish off under the card with a through stitch and knot—or with a bead of glue.

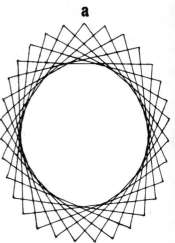

a

A different sequence of sewing will make a different pattern.

You can sew into or out of the first shape you marked, planning your own arrangement of dots from the start.

2 Free stitching

Use a piece of card or thick paper, and a contrasting coloured thread.

Thread the needle and knot the thread.

Start from behind the card; sew a free pattern of stitches across it. The interest will be in the length and direction of the stitches. They can meet, cross and re-cross in a variety of ways. Finish off under the card with a through stitch and knot—or with a bead of glue.

Card (paper)
Craft knife (scissors)
Thread
Needle

Glue

3 Thread print

a Prepare a card of curve or free stitching (1), (2).
(i) Make a roll-through print (p. 176).
(ii) Ink it and make a print (p. 175).

See above, 1, 2

b Glue a free design of thread on a piece of cardboard.

Cardboard, thread
Craft knife (scissors)
Adhesive, spreader

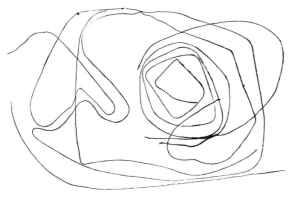

Thread print

When it is quite dry:
(i) Make a roll-through print (p. 176).
(ii) Ink it and make a print (p. 175).

c Lay pieces of thread in any order on a board. Make a roll-through print (p. 176), letting the threads move under the paper if they happen to do so. You will get an 'accidental' design of line and texture. With experience you could control the effect of this more.

Board

4 Thread rubbing

a Prepare a card of curve or free stitching (1) (2). Make a rubbing (p. 179).

See above, 1, 2

b Glue a free design of thread on a piece of cardboard. Let it dry thoroughly. Make a rubbing (p. 179).

Cardboard
Craft knife (scissors)

5 Thread drawing

Soak a length of thread in ink and flake it down freely on a sheet of paper. Lay another sheet of paper over the first. Hold it down flat under a board and draw the thread out towards you with different movements from the 'sandwich' of paper. There will be a line and tone 'drawing' on both pieces of paper. With experience, you can control the effects more.

You can add to the design of marks by re-inking the thread and repeating the process.

Paper, ink, board

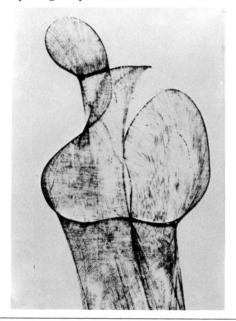

Thread drawing

TILES

Use any kind of glazed or unglazed tile – the sort used for floors, kitchen and bathroom walls, fire surrounds, window sills, roofs, splash boards of old wash-stands.

There will be a range of flat but lovely colours among the unglazed tiles, and a range of bright colours and patterns among the glazed ones. Use from as wide a range as possible.

You may be able to persuade a local builder or tile works to let you have broken or chipped ones cheaply – or ones on which the glaze is imperfect. You may find a good use for them.

Cut the thicker quarry tiles with a cold chisel and hammer – the thinner glazed ones with a glass cutter. Use other related materials if you need to.

Cold chisel, hammer,
(glass cutter)
(Slate, flat marble e.g. off old washstands, flat stones)

1 Tile mosaic

Break or shape tiles into small, squarish pieces (they can be glazed or unglazed depending on the effect you want).
Arrange them into a design.
(i) Make a simple panel mosaic (p. 167).
(ii) Make a plaster bed mosaic (p. 168).

Tools, see above

2 Tile relief

Use whole or broken tiles of any kind or shape. Do any further shaping and trimming needed.
Arrange them into a design.
(i) Make a simple panel relief (p. 167).
(ii) Make a plaster bed relief (p. 168).
NB In both the above, 1 and 2, keep the work fairly small unless you have means to handle and mount heavy panels. With this material, even a small increase in size can add considerably to the final weight.

Tools, see above

3 Tile construction

Use whole or broken tiles of any kind or shape.
Do any further shaping and trimming that you need, and assemble them to make a standing construction, fixing the tiles one at a time with tile cement or glue. You may want to reinforce the construction with cement or fondu (U.S.: Sacrete) if its size or shape needs it. How, when, and where you use it will of course depend on the plans you have for the construction. You may need to set up an arrangement of boards as temporary walls for it (shuttering).

Tools, see above
Adhesive, spreader

Cement (fondu, cement mix), sand, bowl (board, shovel)

Boards and tools

4 Tile – other uses

a As an inking plate for the various print making processes. Use a flat glazed tile.

b As a surface for making a monoprint.

c As a small mixing palette for oil and other kinds of painting.

d As a flat, smooth surface for pouring plaster on if you make a plaster engraving or print.

TIN CANS

Use any suitable kind or size of tin can:
soup, vegetable, fruit, meat, milk drink, soft drink, beer, sweet, jam, syrup, mustard, pet food, tobacco, house and powder paint, car oil.
Clean them well.
Hammer down any sharp edges left by an opener.

Tin opener, hammer

1 Tin can relief

a Use cans on end either way up, with or without lids. Arrange them side by side to make a design of their different heights and their open or closed ends. The lids themselves could form part of the design.
Cut a panel.

Chipboard (blockboard, wood), saw

Paint the cans or the panel if needed, though you will have considered the value of the metal surfaces themselves in the overall effect.

Paint—emulsion, oil or house paint may be best

Punch one or two holes in the bottom of each can or lid, and screw them to the panel in the arrangement decided. (The reason for using screws is that you can get to them with a long screwdriver where you would have difficulty nailing.) If the can is faced downwards with no flat part meeting the panel, you may need to glue a block of wood in first to which to screw it. Though if the cans were light enough you could glue them straight to the panel.

Punch, hammer, screws, awl, screwdriver

Wood block, adhesive, spreader

The effect of the relief can be varied by the addition of other materials. These may also cover screw heads you don't want to show.

Cardboard, wood, other metal, fabric, sand, other texturing material— with adhesive

b Cut down into cans with straight or curving cuts, giving them a new shape.
Arrange them and make a relief (1a).

Tin snips
See above, 1a

c Cut the ends off cans and flatten out the sides that are left. Working on a stout bench, hammer them into new curving or angled shapes. You may need a shaped block of wood to hammer them over.

Tin snips, tin can opener, hammer (mallet)

Wood block

Arrange them together to make a design of their surfaces, painting any that you need to.

Paint—emulsion, oil or house paint may be best

Cut and surface a panel to mount them on.

Chipboard (blockboard, wood), saw, texturing material with adhesive

Punch or drill small holes in the tin strips at suitable points and pin them in place to the panel.

Punch (metal drill), panel pins

d Use lids on their own (there are all kinds).
Arrange and make a relief (1a), but you could use panel pins or finishing nails instead of screws if preferred. Or glue.

See above, 1a
Panel pins or finishing nails, hammer (adhesive, spreader)

e Hammer some cans into different shapes. You could cut some down first if needed.
Arrange them into a flat design.
Cut a panel the right shape.

Hammer, tin snips

Chipboard (blockboard, wood), saw

Punch or drill small holes in each piece of tin at suitable fixing points and nail them onto the panel.
Paint the cans or panel or both, if needed.

Punch (metal drill), nails (panel pins)
Paint—emulsion, oil or house paint may be best

2 Tin can mosaic

Cut the ends (and any rims) off the cans and flatten out the sides that are left.
Cut these into small squarish shapes, not all the same

Tin snips, tin can opener, hammer (mallet)

size. Colour some of them with transparent oil paint so that the metal continues to shine through. Allow time for the paint to dry thoroughly.

Alizarin crimson, ultramarine, prussian blue, monastral blue, viridian, raw sienna, burnt sienna

(i)   Make a simple panel mosaic (p. 167).
(ii) Make a plaster skimmed panel mosaic (p. 170).

3 Tin can sculpture

a Use different kinds of cans.
Arrange and build them as they are to make a standing, hanging or projecting form. They can be end to end, side by side, or side to end.
Join meeting surfaces:
Wire them to each other through punched or drilled holes.

Punch, hammer (metal drill), wire, pliers

Screw them through punched or drilled holes into wood blocks or into a wood framework made to support them. You may want to conceal the wood support, or arrange for it to play an active part in the overall sculpture.

Wood blocks (wood), saw, nails, hammer, screws, punch and hammer (metal drill), awl, screwdriver

Solder them together, or glue them. Meeting surfaces must be quite clean.

Cold solder (solder with soldering iron), or adhesive, spreader
Cleaning agent, emery paper

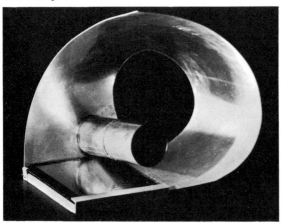

Paint the final construction if needed.

Tin can sculpture
Paint—emulsion, oil or house paint may be best
Hammer (mallet)

b Hammer a can from different sides to make a new shape.
Paint any of the resulting surfaces needed.

Paint—emulsion, oil or house paint may be best
Hammer (mallet)

c Hammer a number of different shaped cans to make new shapes.
Arrange and build them to make a standing, hanging or projecting form, **a**.

See above, a

d Make a relief or form using any combination of tin cans and lids treated in the ways mentioned above, 1, 2, 3.

See above, 1, 2, 3

4 Tin can print

a Cut the ends cleanly out of a smallish can. Hammer out any ragged edges.

Tin snips, can opener
Hammer

Tin can printing

Mix some paint.

Powder paint (emulsion paint), paper, thumb tacks

Lay a large sheet of paper on the table and pin it down. Place the can on it, end down. Keep it pressed down and pour the paint into it. Still keeping it down, move it in different directions: the paint will sweep in broad bands of colour. If there is any paint left inside the tin when the action (and the design) ends, draw it to the edge of·the table and into a bowl held underneath.

Bowl

Exactly the same kind of design can be made on stretched fabric. Pin it to a board covered with newspaper, and use dye instead of paint. You can thicken dye if needed with extender (U.K.: Polycell) though this will affect any fastness of the dye if it is washed afterwards.

Fabric, thumb tacks, board, newspaper
Dye, extender (Polycell) if needed
Bowl

b Cut the flat side from a can.
Tap out any bumps or dents.
Make a monoprint (p. 177).

Tin snips, tin opener
Hammer (mallet)

c Cut the flat side from a can.
Tap out any bumps or dents. Lay it on a piece of wood or board.
Hammer nails to make a design of the dot impressions. Use either the dented or the raised side.
(i) Make a roll-through print (p. 176).
(ii) Ink and make a print (p. 175).

Tin snips, tin opener
Hammer (mallet)
Wood (board)
Nails

5 Tin cans–other uses

a Make a palette for holding dry powder paint.
Use small (pet food) tin cans, the same size. Make sure the lids are off clean, with no sharp, jagged edges.
Arrange a number of them (say 6, 8 or 9) side by side into a square or rectangle.

Tin opener, hammer

Cut a shape of chipboard a little bigger than this.

Chipboard, saw

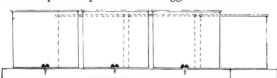

Tin can palette

Punch a small hole in the bottom of each can and screw it into place on the board (this will not hold wet paint, of course).

Punch (metal drill), small screws, awl, screwdriver

Paint the cans with emulsion or house paint to cut down any rusting.

Emulsion paint (house paint)

b Use a lid as a bed for a small plaster mosaic.

c Use a can as a water container. Treat it as above, **a**.

TISSUE PAPER

There is a very wide range of both rich and subtle colours in tissue paper. They have richness of their own. Usually, however, they are not light-fast, and the colour runs if they are wetted.
This should be kept in mind when planning work (the colour running can, in fact, be put to use at times).

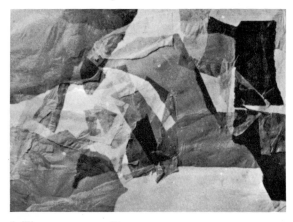

Tissue paper collage. Child

1 Tissue paper collage

a Tear or cut tissue papers into different shapes, and paste them to paper or cardboard to make a design. You will find it easier to paste the paper or card you are mounting them on. Make use of any colour flooding.
The papers will become transparent when they are wet, but they will lose this when they are dry again.

Paper (cardboard), scissors (craft knife), paste, bowl, flat brush

b To bring out and keep the rich, transparent quality of the tissue colours, stick them down with a clear varnish, polyurethane or acrylic (U.S.): brush some varnish on the card; lay the tissue on it, and go over it again with the brush to work it flat. Different layers of tissue will build up to a deeper colour effect, and all the layers used will play a part in the final top colour.

Paper (cardboard), scissors (craft knife), clear varnish (polyurethane or acrylic), flat brush

c Shred, crumple or twist up coloured tissues.
Cut a piece of paper or cardboard and stick the tissue pieces to it to make a design of their contrasting textures and colours. The pieces can be spaced, close together, or built up.

Paper (cardboard), scissors (craft knife)
Adhesive, spreader

2 Tissue paper windows

Cut an arrangement of holes in a shape of cardboard. Paint the face of the cardboard if needed.
Turn the cardboard, face down. Tear coloured tissues and paste them across the holes. The colours can overlap quite freely. Lift the cardboard from time to time to see how the overlapping is affecting the colours.
Set the finished tissue paper window against the light.

Cardboard, craft knife, powder paint (emulsion paint)
Adhesive, spreader

TWIGS AND SMALL BRANCHES

1 Twig collage/relief

Use a variety of twigs. Cut or strip them to lie as flat as possible.
Arrange them to lie close or spaced to make a design of their formations and colours.
Make a collage (p. 165) or a simple panel relief (p. 167).

Craft knife, penknife, secateurs, garden shears

2 Twig carving

Examine a twig for a shape already present in it suggested by its growth formation.
Whittle it to bring out this shape more clearly. Use any simple cutting tool.
You can of course combine other carved twigs or other materials with it to arrive at the shape you want. Glue, slot, wire or fix these in any way suitable.

Penknife, craft knife, small file, sandpaper

Adhesive, spreader
Wire, pliers, awl (wood drill)

3 Twig painting

Use a suitable twig, whole or shaped, as a painting tool with thicker paints.

Craft knife
Paint and painting surface

4 Twig construction

Shape and build up twigs to make a standing, hanging or projecting construction.
Use glue or fine wire to join them.

Introduce colour if needed.

Craft knife, penknife, secateurs or shears
Adhesive, spreader
Wire, pliers, awl (wood drill)
Powder paint (emulsion paint)

Branch carving. Student

Twig painting

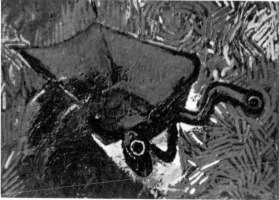

VEGETABLES

Some vegetables you may find useful:
potato, turnip, swede, kohl rabi, carrot, broad bean,
pea, sprout, parsnip, onion, sugar beet.
There will certainly be others you can think of and will
want to try.
They will not all be equally useful–or even suitable–
for every craft. You will know which ones can be used.
You can combine other plant forms with them for any
special effects you need.

1 Vegetable study

Make a study of the shape, colour, texture and growth
of vegetables, using any suitable material or process.

· Materials, tools as needed

2 Vegetable carving

Use a firm vegetable (see above).
Carve it with any simple tool to make a shape.

Craft knife, penknife,
gouge, kitchen knife,
apple corer, nail

You could mount the finished carving on a cocktail stick
(or similar) fixed in another half vegetable.

Cocktail stick

3 Vegetable modelling

Shape and combine suitable vegetables with other
materials to make a model.

Shaping tools (see above)
Thin wood, metal or hard
plastic pieces, nails, wire,
matches, fabric, various scrap,
with tools

Fix them together by slotting, wiring, stringing or any
other means suggested by the vegetables.

Wire, pliers (string, scissors),
awl

4 Vegetable puppet

Other tools, adhesive

Shape and combine suitable vegetables with other
materials to make a puppet.

Shaping tools, see above, 2

Fix them together, see above, 3 or by simple means like
cloth hinges and pins.

Tools, see above, 3

You can make a simple string puppet worked from a
wood cross-piece, or a puppet fixed to a rod for stage or
shadow shows.
These puppets are short-lived, of course.

Wood, wire, string,
dowelling, with tools

5 Vegetable print

You can make prints with most of the vegetables listed.
Halve or slice them, and make prints from their flat
surfaces (p. 175), though some of the softer ones like
sprouts will have a short printing life. Others, like
onions, will tend to come apart after a while. But while
they last, they make their own special marks.

Kitchen knife

You can make all-over patterns, printing freely to create
a design with the halved vegetable as it is. Or with firmer
vegetables you can cut and gouge into the surface to
make a more involved pattern.

Craft knife, penknife,
gouge

WALLPAPER

Wallpaper collage

Use odd lengths of wallpaper and old wallpaper sample books.

1 Wallpaper collage

Use wallpaper pieces that have interesting colour, pattern or texture qualities.
Tear or cut them into different shapes.   Scissors
Make a collage (p. 165).

2 Wallpaper mosaic

Tear or cut contrasting coloured or textured wallpapers   Scissors
into small squarish pieces.
Make a simple panel mosaic (p. 167).

3 Wallpaper print

Tear or cut out shapes of wallpaper with contrasting   Scissors
and pronounced relief texture (the range of embossed
papers).
Glue them to cardboard to make a design of these   Cardboard, craft knife,
contrasts.   adhesive, spreader
(i)   Make a roll-through print (p. 176).
(ii) Ink and make a print (p. 175).
These textures will soon flatten and their printing life is
limited.

WAX

Use paraffin wax, candle wax or similar.
Be careful of fire risk in the following. Keep the wax away
from direct heat. Melt it in a double saucepan or a tin   Double saucepan or
can in a pan of water. Form a lip in the tin can (like a   tin can, pan
jug) for pouring.

1 Wax modelling

a Heat wax and let it drip into a free-fall shape, building up like a stalagmite – or flowing into a broader shape, just for the feel of it. You may be able to make something of it by controlled dripping; or it may give you ideas for more permanent work.

Board, tin can, pan

b Make a small model of twisted wire. It can either stand by itself or be fixed to a base, e.g. by staples into a wood block.
Heat the wax and drip it onto the wire, covering as much of it as you want to. The twists in the wire will hold the wax.
You can smooth the finished form if needed with a warmed knife.

Wire, pliers
(Wood block, staples, hammer or staple gun)
Tin can, pan

Knife

2 Wax resist

a On paper.
Lay a sheet of paper flat on a board.
Melt wax with a little white spirit, and keep it warm during use.
Paint a design with wax on the paper.
Wash over the design with water colour or thinned powder paint. The wax will resist the colour and remain as a contrasting design.
If the wax is rather thick, you can iron it out through a sheet of brown paper, which will draw and absorb the wax.

Paper, board
Tin can, pan
Brush
Water colour (powder paint)

Flat iron, brown paper, newspaper

b On fabric.
(i) Stretch a piece of fabric over newspaper on a board and pin it down (the newspaper padding will prevent wax spoiling the board).
Melt wax as above, **a**.
Paint a design with wax on the fabric.
Repeat the design on the back.
Mix some cold water dye. Immerse the fabric and leave it in the dye for several minutes. There will be instructions about this on most commercial dye drums.
Lay the dipped fabric on a padded table (more newspaper will do for this). Cover the fabric with brown paper and go over it with a flat iron. The brown paper will draw and absorb the wax, leaving the design clear on the dyed fabric.
(ii) Prepare a piece of fabric and the wax as above, (i).
Paint wax boldly over the fabric. Let it dry, and crumple it in both hands. Dip it in the dye as above. Take it out

Fabric, newspaper, board, thumb tacks

Tin can, pan, brush

Cold water dye, bowl

Brown paper, flat iron

See above, (i)

Cold water dye, bowl

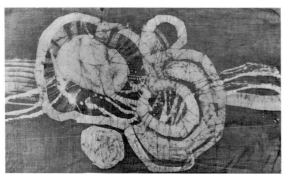

Wax resist. Student

and iron it as above. There will be a crackle design across the areas where the wax broke up. You can repeat the process with other colours for a different effect.

Brown paper, flat iron

3 Wax carving

Use a block of paraffin wax – or melt it down and pour it into a temporary mould nearer the shape you want to carve from, e.g. a firm carton.
Carve it in your hands with any suitable tool.
A warmed blade will produce a different kind of surface.

Can, pan

Carton
Craft knife, pen knife, hacksaw blade, small kitchen knife

4 Wax – other uses

a Use wax for casting from a simple mould that can be removed easily afterwards, e.g. plasticine.

b Use wax for resisting colour applied to areas in other crafts, e.g. colouring a flat plaster cast.

WAX CRAYONS

1 Wax crayon etching

Use big wax crayons and a piece of cartridge (or heavy, drawing) paper, or a paper of similar quality.
Crayon all over the paper with one or more colours, pressing fairly hard to get a dense effect. Then go over the surface again with one or more different coloured crayons (alternatively, and perhaps easier, paint over the first waxed surface with a mixture of dry powder colour in a little liquid detergent, and allow it to dry thoroughly).
Now you can etch through this top layer with a pointed tool to expose the contrasting colours beneath.
Make your design.

Cartridge paper or similar

Powder colour, liquid detergent, small container

Chip of wood, metal, hard plastic, nail, nail file, old ball-point pen

2 Wax crayon resist

Draw with a wax crayon on any white or coloured paper. Mix a different coloured paint (water colour, thinned powder paint) and wash over the crayon drawing. The wax crayon marks will resist the wash and remain in contrast. Some combinations of crayon, paper and wash will be clearer than others.

Paper
Water colour (powder paint)

3 Wax crayon – other uses

a As a drawing medium in its own right.

b As a medium for making rubbings (p. 179).

c As a decorative element in plaster casts. Melt down the old ends of crayons and pour into the cavities of a cast or relief.

WIRE

1 Wire relief

Cut and bend various kinds of wire to make a design.
Make a simple panel relief (p. 167).
You may want to use other materials with the wire for
contrast.

Pliers (side cutters)

(Perforated zinc, metal gauze,
punched bar, machine
components, metal turnings)

2 Wire modelling

Use a fairly flexible wire (gauge 16 or 18 perhaps) in
manageable lengths: join lengths as you need to by
twisting them tightly together with pliers, binding them
with finer wire, soldering, or glueing them.
Use other materials with the wire if needed.

Pliers (side cutters)
or Cold solder (solder with
soldering iron)
or Adhesive, spreader
Tools, see above

a Bend the wire to make a flat shape to stand, hang or
project. If you are standing it, you may need a base of
wood or other material, e.g. a suitable piece of metal or
machine scrap.

Wood block, awl (wood drill)
Other material

b Bend the wire to make a three-dimensional shape to
stand, hang or project.

Tools, see above

c Bend the wire as above, **b**, but keep the parts fairly
close together: join parts by twisting.
(i) Mix plaster (p. 172) and drip it onto the wire model,
letting it build up to the form you want.
Model the surface further if you need to.

Tools, see above

Knife, chip of wood, metal,
hard plastic, plaster rasp,
riffler, nail file

Wire and metal modelling. Student

Colour the plaster if needed (p. 173).
(ii) Melt paraffin or candle wax and drip onto the wire
model, letting it build up to the form you want.
Model the surface further if you need to. A warmed
knife is useful for this.

Paraffin wax (candle wax),
tin can, pan
Knife

d Bend the wire to make a three-dimensional shape to
stand, hang or project.
(i) Mix delayed setting plaster (p. 173) or cellulose
filler.
Cut butter muslin or cheesecloth, or a similar material

Tools, see above

Plaster with size (cellulose
filler), bowl
Butter muslin or cheesecloth,
scissors

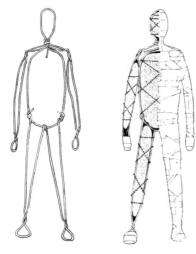

Wire and parcel modelling

into strips, soak them in the plaster and wrap them round the wire model to build up the form. As it dries, model further plaster onto the surface to complete it if needed; but don't overload this.

(ii) Tear newspaper into strips, soak them in paste and wrap them round the wire model to build up the form. Both the above can be painted when they are dry.

Palette knife (spatula, kitchen knife)
Newspaper, paste, bowl

Ink (dye, powder paint, emulsion paint)

e Wire and parcel modelling.
Use a medium thickness wire (about gauge 18), a few feet long. Form it into a shape with each of the main parts made up of a loop.

Tools, see above

Crumple newspaper into compact 'parcels' and work them into the wire loops. Bind them into place with fine twine or wire (florists' wire is useful).

Newspaper
Twine (fine wire), scissors

Soak strips of newspaper in paste, and lay them over and round the parcels, working them into place with both hands (hold the model bodily!). Continue laying and binding strips to fill out the surface form. You can model it further by crumpling more paper, building it on, and pasting strips across it as before.

Paste, bowl

When the form is finished, let it dry (it may take a day or so) and paint or texture it with suitable materials depending on the effect you want.

Powder paint (emulsion paint), texturing materials with adhesive

3 Wire print

Cut lengths of thin wire.
Arrange them *flat* to make a design. Don't cross the wires over each other.

Pliers (side cutters)

Cut a shape of board and glue the wire to it.
When it is quite dry:

Board, saw
Adhesive, spreader

(i) Make a roll-through print (p. 176).
(ii) Ink it and make a print (p. 175).
These will be line prints. If you want to add tone or texture areas you can use sand, or similar material, and glue it to the board (see p. 166).

Texturing material with adhesive

This is now an uneven surface. Make an uneven-surface print (p. 176).
Note. The panel may look very attractive as a relief in its own right when you have finished with the printing. The ink will have given it colour.

4 Wire plaster cast

Make a wire relief (1); or a print surface (3). Or use old ones you no longer need.
See above, 1, 3
Make a plaster cast of it (p. 174).
Colour the cast if needed (p. 174).
If you are using an old print surface, you may find the colour remaining on it transfers a little to the plaster. This can be quite pleasing.

WOOD

Wood carving

Use any reasonably soft, dry wood to start with, just to get the feel of a chisel and mallet.
Some suitable woods: Balsa, North American yellow pine, lime, cedar, birch. Some harder woods: pear, oak, yew, cherry, sycamore, maple, walnut, mahogany, teak. But it is the character of a piece of wood that makes it easy or tough to carve: some hard woods are better to work than some soft woods.
All wood has its own distinct qualities of colour, grain, texture and weight, and these will play an important part in how you carve it.
Some woods work well with short bevels on the tools; others work well with longer ones.

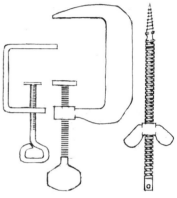

Cramps (clamps) and bench screw

a Carving in the round.
You will need to secure the wood in a clamp of some kind, or keep it steady by other means. You can use an ordinary bench vice, a G-cramp (U.S.: C-clamp) (which screws up tight round the edge of the bench), or a bench screw (screws up through a hole in the bench into the carving block). Or you can screw your block to a heavier base of wood and secure *that* to the bench.

Bench vice, G-cramp, C-clamp, bench screw, wood block with screws, awl, screwdriver

Use a few simple tools, say: ½″ chisel, ½″ shallow gouge, ¼″ deep gouge (enlarge the range by adding more shapes and sizes as you can), a beech mallet, a tenon saw or coping saw and an oil stone and sharpening slips to fit your gouges.

½″ chisel, ½″ shallow gouge, ¼″ deep gouge, beech mallet, tenon saw or coping saw, oil stone, slips, oil; X-acto gouges useful in small work

Carve directly into the wood, discovering forms and surface textures as you go, and working towards the idea in mind.
Or make a sketch of the shape you want to carve, then sketch the shape on both sides of the block. Mark the high points you will want to keep with an X and carve away from these to the deeper levels. You can do some preliminary shaping of the block with a saw; then use a chisel or gouge directing it at the angle you find best in relation to the grain or the wood texture. Work with bold cuts, not over-cautious ones. Use the patterns of grain and follow any rhythms exposed that relate to what are carving. Towards the end, you will probably find it enough to use hand pressure alone on the cutting tool. Finish off with sandpaper if you want a smooth surface, though the tool marks are often best left as part of the carving.
In addition to the tools listed, you may like to use other

Wood carving tools

Sandpaper

wood tools you have: spokeshave (pares off the wood in a downward movement), a brace and bit, a craft knife, a wood file.

Keep your tools sharp at all times. Use an oil stone or the right shaped slip, and sharpen to the original angle or bevel of the cutting edge.

Spokeshave, brace and bit, craft knife, wood file

b Carving in relief.

Prepare the face of the wood by planing if needed. Set it up against a bench stop, or in a suitable clamp (see above).

Plane

See above

Carve directly into the wood, discovering relief forms and surface textures as you go, and working towards the idea in mind.

Or draw the design on the wood, marking the high points with an X. Carve from these, down to the deeper levels in carefully controlled stages, watching how light and shadow, and the deeper grain, affect the definition at different levels. Keep the wood turned to the best position for cutting.

Drawing medium

Keep your tools sharp at all times (see above).

Wood carvings. Adult

WOOD BOXES

Use from the many different kinds of boxes that come your way from time to time: seed boxes, apple and orange boxes, crates, tea chests, cigar boxes, old drawers.

1 Wood box construction

Use the boxes as they are, or cut down to new shapes.

Saw

Assemble them to make a large (outdoor?) construction, or a smaller one, depending on the boxes you have. They can be side by side, on top of each other, turned at different angles, upside down, or inside each other. Screw or nail them together.

Screws, awl (wood drill), screwdriver
or
Nails (panel pins or finishing nails), hammer—a claw will probably be most useful

Paint the finished construction if needed.

Paint (emulsion or house oil paint if outdoors)

2 Wood box painting

Tidy up your box. Plane or sandpaper rough parts. Prepare it for painting all round (p. 156). Paint its sides with designs to make a three-dimensional painting.

Saw, hammer, pliers, surform, plane, sandpaper Powder paint (emulsion paint, house oil paint)

3 Wood box—other uses

a For storing scrap and other materials. Mark clearly.

b As painting panels. Remove the ends and sides. Tidy and smooth them as above, 2.

Tools, see above, 2

c As print blocks. Remove the ends and sides. Tidy and smooth them as above, 2. The printing surface should be as smooth as you can make it, though some of the grain texture could well play a part in your print. Use it if you can. Design, cut and make a print (see Wood off-cuts, p. 146).

Tools, see above, 2

WOOD OFF-CUTS AND SCRAPS

Use wood scraps of all kinds and shapes, and from any nearby source: workshop, builders' yard, boat yard, junk yard; from house repair work and your own work with wood in other crafts. Other useful kinds: driftwood, firewood, old fencing.
Wood that has not been painted before should be primed before oil paint is used on it (see p. 156).
Be careful of fire risk in 1 and 2.

1 Wood scrap relief

Use wood pieces with different end and face grain (grain patterns can be strengthened by oiling with linseed or teak oil, or by rubbing in powdered chalk, or by scorching, but care must be taken if this method is used). Colour with wood stain or paint if needed.

Linseed oil (teak oil), chalk, blow lamp or brazing torch (*care here!*), paint (wood stain)

Make a simple panel relief (p. 167).

Scorched wood

Countersink any screwheads you don't want to show (or sink any such nail heads with a punch). Fill in with plastic wood (U.K.: Brummer stopping) or sawdust and glue. Sometimes you may be able to screw through from the back of the panel into the relief pieces.

Countersink (punch, hammer)
Plastic wood (U.K.: Brummer stopping) (glue)

2 Wood scrap scorch design

Use a fair sized piece of wood.
Mask certain parts of it with flat metal, e.g. cut from opened-out cans. Tap a few panel pins or finishing nails into the wood round the edge of the metal shapes, and raise the panel as near upright as you can.
Play a blow lamp or brazing torch to scorch the exposed areas to different depths, making a design of lightly, deeply and un-charred wood. Be careful of fire hazard. Remove excess charring with wire wool or sandpaper as you go.

Metal sheeting, tin snips
Panel pins or finishing nails, hammer

Blow lamp (brazing torch)

Wire wool (sandpaper)

3 Wood scrap construction

Assemble wood pieces to make a construction to stand, hang or project. Fix them together with screws, nails, glue, or by jointing–or by a combination of these.
Use the natural wood colours and grain, or colour with wood stain or paint.

Saw
Screws, awl (wood drill), screwdriver
or Nails (panel pins or finishing nails), hammer
or Adhesive, spreader
or Chisel, mallet
Wood stain (paint)

4 Wood scrap rubbing

Make a rubbing of the grain of wood scraps (p. 179). Tear out selected rubbings and combine them to make a new design. Paste them to a suitable mount.

Paste, bowl
Paper (cardboard), craft knife

5 Wood scrap print

a Use a flat piece of wood that has a prominent grain. Ink it and make a print (p. 175). If the print of the grain suggests a possible design (look at it all ways up) cut into the block with a suitable tool to develop the design as you see it.

Craft knife, X-acto gouge, linoleum cutter, wood gouge

Wood print. Child

Ink and make a second print. Continue in this way
until you have the effect you want.

b Use a flat piece of wood that has a smooth face.
Make it as smooth as you can. Finish with a very fine
sand- or flour-paper.
Draw a design lightly on the wood.
Engrave the lines, holding the cutter at the best angle
to make the kind of cut you want and without tearing
the grain. Use a craft knife to make V-shaped cuts,
working from either side at 45°. Use a gouge to texture
or clear other areas.
Ink and make a print (p. 175).
In both the above, **a** and **b**, you may want a small
G-cramp (U.S.: C-clamp) to hold the wood steady
as you are cutting.

Sandpaper round a small
wood block
Drawing medium
Craft knife, X-acto gouge,
wood gouge, linoleum cutter

G-cramp, clamp

c Use the natural face and end grain (and the edges) of
different small wood pieces as print 'tools'.
Make a print (p. 175), repeating it in various ways to
build up a design. Use as many pieces or colours as
needed.

d Use a piece of wood with a close-grained face.
Lay different metal objects on it, and hammer them in
to make sharp, clear impressions, removing each one
afterwards.
Ink the block and make a print (p. 175). The impressions will form a contrasting design.

Hammer
Nail, screw, wire, machine
part, scrap metal

6 Wood scrap painting

Use a wood off-cut to paint on.
Prepare it for painting if needed, e.g. smoothing or
priming.
Design on one or more sides to make a three-dimensional
painting. (A number of these could be grouped together:
it would be well to plan this first.)

(Sandpaper block, emulsion
paint)
Powder paint (emulsion
paint, other paint)

MATERIALS AND TOOLS

Most of these materials are available in artists' supply shops, hardware stores, ironmongers and stationers, builders' supply companies or decorators' shops. They are supplied under various trade names, and I recommend that you check with your local suppliers who should be in a position to advise the best materials for the projects you have in mind.

ADHESIVES

Wherever an adhesive is needed in the following activities, you should use the paste, gum or glue that is most suitable. The Table of Adhesives (p. 150) indicates which these are, in respect of each of the main materials you are likely to meet.

You will also need a spreader. This can be a paste or glue brush, a plastic spreader, the container itself in some cases, or an improvised tool.

If you are mixing up a cold water paste, you will also need a bowl. If you are making hot water glue, you will need a glue pot or a similar melting container. These are not mentioned separately each time in the text.

Cold water paste. Just add the paste powder to the water slowly, stirring as you do so, until you have the right consistency—not too thick, not too thin.

Cellulose paste. A little of this goes a long way: read the quantities recommended on the package carefully. Add the powder to the water slowly, stirring for a minute. Stir again from time to time during the next 15 minutes until the specks in the mixture have dissolved. This paste will keep for several days without deterioration.

Melting glue

Hot water glue (known as Scotch glue). In the form of flat cakes, pellets or powder. Sold by weight.

Soak it for a while in cold water, then heat it, in more water if needed, in a glue pot or a similar kind of container. A tin can in a pan of water will do.

Use it hot.

Glue or mucilage in a tube, tin can or jar.

There are general-purpose glues for most light-weight jobs involving paper, card, light fabrics, etc.

There are stronger glues for jobs involving heavier materials and for sticking the increasing range of new materials like plastic. The instructions on the container will generally tell you the range of materials that the glue will stick, together with advice about how to use it. It is well worth reading these.

Adhesives to stick the material to other materials

	Scotch Super Strength	Scotch Epoxy	Scotch Contact	Scotch Wood and Paper	Scotch Construction	Scotch Spra-ment
Asbestos					☐	
Bone		☐				
Brick					☐	
Cane	☐		☐			
Canvas			☐	☐		
Cement block					☐	
China	☐					
Concrete					☐	
Cork				☐		☐
Corrugated cardboard	☐			☐		☐
Egg shell				☐		
Fabric			☐	☐		☐
Film negative	☐		☐			
Foam plastic			☐			☐
Formica			☐			
Glass	☐	☐				
Hardboard or Masonite			☐	☐	☐	
Leather	☐		☐			
Linoleum			☐			
Metal	☐	☐	☐			
Metal foil			☐			☐
Nylon		☐				
Plaster					☐	
Plastic	☐					
Plastic Laminates			☐			
Polystyrene (expanded)				☐	☐	☐
Polythene						☐
Phonograph Records	☐		☐			
Rubber			☐			
Slate					☐	
Stone		☐			☐	
Terra cotta		☐				
Tiles (glazed)					☐	
Tiles (unglazed)				☐	☐	
Vinyl	☐					
Wood		☐	☐	☐	☐	

Note: The Publishers wish to acknowledge the technical assistance of the 3 M Company in compiling this chart. There are of course numerous adhesive brand names on the market and your art supply dealer will be able to suggest corresponding products which will do the job of the Scotch adhesives recommended here for a particular material.

Adhesives to stick the material to itself

	Scotch Super Strength	Scotch Epoxy	Scotch Contact	Scotch Wood and Paper	Scotch Construction	Scotch Spra-ment
Asbestos					□	
Bone		□				
Brick					□	
Cane			□			
Canvas			□			
Cement block					□	
China		□				
Concrete					□	
Cork						□
Corrugated cardboard				□		□
Egg shell						
Fabric				□		□
Film negative		□				
Foam plastic			□			□
Formica			□			
Glass	□	□				
Hardboard or Masonite			□	□	□	
Leather		□	□			
Linoleum			□			
Metal		□	□			
Metal foil			□			□
Nylon		□				
Plaster					□	
Plastic		□				
Plastic Laminates			□			
Polystyrene (expanded)						□
Polythene						□
Phonograph Records	□		□			
Rubber			□			
Slate					□	
Stone		□			□	
Terra cotta		□				
Tiles (glazed)		□				
Tiles (unglazed)				□	□	
Vinyl		□				
Wood		□	□		□	

Some trade-named adhesives have different numbers or names for different uses, and you should check that you are using the one recommended.

Gum, prepared paste. For use with lighter weight materials when a slightly stronger bond is wanted than that given by ordinary paste.

BOARDS

There are many different kinds of board. Use the kind that seems right for the job:

Blockboard. Laminated wood strips, faced on both sides with wood ply.

Chipboard. Made of compressed wood chippings. It is very useful if you want a board of some size that will take nails and screws like wood, can be sawn, and will not warp or split.

Chipboard faced with formica.

Hardboard or Masonite.

Insulation board. This comes in several qualities and thicknesses, and is sold under various trade names (U.K. Sundealer, Celotex). It is softer than hardboard in texture, and will take ordinary pins. But it is quite strong and rigid.

Marine plywood. The layers and laminations do not peel apart when they are wet.

Pegboard. A perforated hardboard.

Plywood. 5-ply or 7-ply are probably most useful.

Timber.

Crates.

Fruit boxes e.g. orange, apple .

Packing cases.

Panels from old furniture, e.g. sideboards, table tops, cupboards, wardrobes.

Tea chests.

BRUSHES

Different jobs need different brushes. It will help to refer back to this note if you are in doubt.

Brushes are sold in a range of sizes indicated by numbers (0–12 as a rule, i.e. small to large) or by width (1″–4″ for most purposes).

There are also different shapes: pointed, round, flat, and filbert (tapered).

a   Brushes to paint with

Bristle brushes. These are stiff, and can have long or short handles. They are generally made of hog-bristle, and are good for bold, free work.

Hair brushes. These are softer, and can have long or short handles. They are mostly made of squirrel, bear, ox or sable

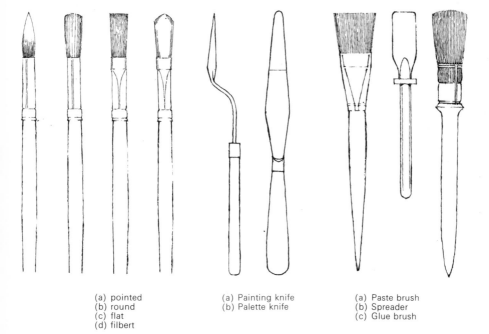

(a) pointed
(b) round
(c) flat
(d) filbert

(a) Painting knife
(b) Palette knife

(a) Paste brush
(b) Spreader
(c) Glue brush

hair—squirrel being the cheapest and sable the dearest.

Decorators' brushes. These can be stiff or soft, and are useful for bigger work. They are used for house painting, after all!

Note. A painting or palette knife is useful for different effects. It can be made of metal or plastic—or you could make one yourself from thin scrap (metal, plastic, wood).

b   Brushes to paste with

Any of the brushes mentioned above will do, though you would probably not want to use the more expensive ones. There are also special flat paste brushes, often made of nylon.

c   Brushes to glue with

Bristle brushes, as above.

Decorators' brushes, as above.

Special round glue brushes. These are wired as a reinforcement, and are certainly the best if you are using hot water glue for big areas.

Note. You can also use a plastic spreader for some glues. It is cheap and often does the job better than a brush. It is easier to clean too.

Clean all brushes thoroughly.

After using them with any water-based paint or with paste, clean them with water.

After using them with any oil-based paint, clean them with turps substitute or paraffin.

After using them with a hot water glue, clean them with warm water.

Don't leave them standing on their bristles.

CARDBOARD

There are many different kinds of cardboard. Use the kind that seems right for the job:

Bristol Board. A thin cardboard, usually white.

Corrugated cardboard. In rolls. Yellow or grey and some other colours.

Manilla. A light-weight, smooth card in a range of colours.

Millboard. A tough, rigid board. Grey.

Pasteboard. A smooth, strong mounting board. White and coloured.

Strawboard. A heavy, rigid board. Straw coloured.

The thickness of the cardboard is indicated either by weight, or by the number of sheets in it, e.g. 3-sheet, 6-sheet.

Other useful kinds of cardboard:

Boxes.

Cartons.

Display boards.

Packing boards.

CLAY

This is supplied in powdered or plastic form. The plastic clay is ready to use.

There are several kinds of clay prepared by suppliers; they include:

Grey clay. Fires buff or white.

Red clay. Fires red.

Crank mixture. A grogged clay, coarser to handle.

Clay is sold by the lb. or in 1 cwt. packs, and needs to be stored in air-tight bins or in plastic bags when you are not using it.

There are also some made-up modelling clays, sold under trade names (U.K. Alostone). These have their own special qualities of texture and setting.

Note. You can, of course, dig and prepare your own clay if you prefer. For further help in this, see p. 36.

COLOURS

Try to build up a good selection of colours in any kind of medium you use. It will give you greater choice and make mixing more exciting.

There will be colours you especially like, and these are often the best ones to start your collection with. But a first selection might look something like this (though the colour names vary a little between different makers):

Powder paint	Oil paint, acrylic or polymer paint
Scarlet	Cadmium red
Vermilion	Vermilion
Crimson	Crimson Alizarin
Brilliant yellow	Cadmium yellow
Gamboge	Chrome yellow
Lemon	Lemon yellow

Ultramarine	Ultramarine
Prussian blue	Prussian blue
Turquoise	Monastral blue
Viridian	Cerulean
Emerald	Viridian
Terre verte	Emerald
Burnt sienna	Terre verte
Burnt umber	Burnt sienna
Yellow ochre	Burnt umber
Black	Yellow ochre, golden ochre
White	Ivory black
	Titanium or flake white

Pastels and crayons have similar names.

There is also a range of Ostwald (U.K.) colours which are standardised, and are known as Ostwald red, yellow, blue, etc., and the Munsell scale of colours (U.S.A.).

In house painters' emulsion and oil paints, the colours usually have other names. You will want to choose from the manufacturer's colour chart.

Some colours are permanent under most conditions; others are more likely to fade or change for different reasons over a period of time. You can check on this from the makers' catalogue generally, but either way, most colours today are surprisingly durable, and this aspect need give no trouble normally.

DRAWING MEDIA

Chalk, white and coloured. There is a dustless chalk.

Charcoal. In thin and thick sticks, soft or hard.

Crayons. Conté crayon ⎱ Like a harder pastel
Terrachrome crayon ⎰

Pencil crayon

Wax crayon. In small and large sizes.

Inks. Waterproof drawing inks, in black and white and a wide range of bright transparent colours.

Writing ink.

Pastels soft or hard (there is also an oil pastel).

Pencils of all kinds.

Pens. Felt tip pens. Lots of colours. They make dense, bold lines.

Fibre tip pens. Lots of colours. They make dense, pencil-like lines. (Both these pens are obtainable in smudge-proof or water based ink.)

Writing pens—ball-point, steel nib.

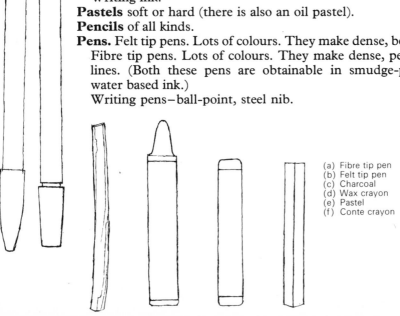

(a) Fibre tip pen
(b) Felt tip pen
(c) Charcoal
(d) Wax crayon
(e) Pastel
(f) Conté crayon

PAINTS

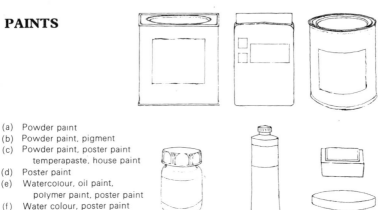

(a) Powder paint
(b) Powder paint, pigment
(c) Powder paint, poster paint
      temperapaste, house paint
(d) Poster paint
(e) Watercolour, oil paint,
      polymer paint, poster paint
(f) Water colour, poster paint

Acrylic or polymer paint

This is a dense, moist paint, similar to oil paint in consistency, but drying faster and capable of different effects. It is in tubes or other containers, or it can be made up by mixing dry colour with a special binder.

Use it undiluted, or thinned a little with water.

Emulsion paint as used by house painters.

This is in liquid or soft paste form, and is in tins.

Use it neat, straight from the tin, or thinned a little with water. The colour dries matt or with a slight sheen. It dries fairly fast.

Oil paint as used by easel painters.

This is a dense, moist paint.

Use it undiluted, straight from the container, or thinned a little with turpentine, or mixed with a drying oil (like linseed) or with wax. It dries with a shine or matt, depending on what you thin or mix it with. This paint will sink into absorbent surfaces and become dull, so prepare the surface first with a wash of size and a coat of underpaint or gesso (whiting and size), a coat of emulsion paint, or a special primer–depending on the surface you are using.

Oil paint as used by house painters.

This is in liquid or soft paste form.

Use it neat, straight from the container, or thinned a little with turps substitute, white spirit or benzine. There is an under-coat paint that dries matt, and a gloss paint that dries shiny.

This paint too will sink into absorbent surfaces, so prepare the surface first as above (if you are painting on new wood, you will probably find it best to use a special wood primer or emulsion paint).

Powder paint, or powder colour.

This is in powder form as the name implies.

Just mix it with water in a palette. The colour is opaque and dries matt.

Wherever powder paint is mentioned in the text, you could use poster paint or temperapaste instead if you wished.

Mix these with water in a palette, or use them undiluted for thicker effect.

Water colour.

This is in moist form in tubes, or is made up into tablets, cakes, or pans.

Just mix it with water. This is the traditional water colour medium and is best used in transparent washes on a white surface, giving the colour its full brilliance.

Note. Whenever paint is mentioned in the text, it is taken to include the following equipment:

A mixing palette

A container for water or other thinner

A brush or brushes—or other painting tools you might like to use, like a painting knife or an improvised spreader

A paint rag, if needed

These will not therefore be listed separately.

You can make up interesting paints yourself by mixing dry colour with other binders. Some you may like to try are a liquid wax (as used for the home or car); a polyurethane sealer, (U.K.: Ronseal); a paste. In fact, almost anything that adheres to a surface, is colourless, and dries, will be worth trying. But you will want to experiment to find the right proportions and discover how quickly and how well it dries.

PALETTES

For keeping dry powder paint in, plastic stacking palettes with six wells are good for most purposes. Mix the colours on a sandwich tin, plate or any large flat pan, or plastic ice cube tray. There is room to enjoy mixing on these.

Use a jar or a tin can for the water.

For mixing oil or polymer paint, use a flat plastic or wood or disposable paper palette, or improvise with a sandwich tin, a piece of formica, or something similar.

Use a big clip-on dipper or oil cup, a jar, or tin can for the thinner.

Stacking palette

PAPERS

a **For drawing and painting.**

Almost any kind of paper is useful and worth trying:

Cartridge paper (U.S.: Heavy drawing paper). Smooth, white drawing paper. Different qualities.

Coloured paper.

Detail paper. Thin and strong. White.

Duplicating paper. Thin and fairly strong. Various colours.

Grey bogus paper (U.S.).

Kitchen paper. Thin. White. A good general purpose paper.

Lining or shelf paper. Thin. White.

Manilla paper.

Newspaper (you can sometimes get blank newsprint).

Pastel or charcoal paper / Sugar paper / (U.S.: Construction paper) — Slightly rough. Lots of colours. Good general papers.

Typing paper. Different thicknesses.

Wall paper. Various textures and colours.

Wrapping paper. Often tough. Brown or grey mostly, though in many interesting colours as well.

b   For printmaking.

Again, almost any kind of paper is useful and will produce different effects, though some are better for certain kinds of printing than others.

You can use any of these papers in the processes mentioned in the text:

Detail paper
Duplicating paper
Imitation Japanese printing paper
Kitchen paper ⎫
Lining or shelf paper ⎬ Good quality preferably
Tissue paper, white or coloured ⎭
Typing paper.

There is, of course, a further wide range of specially prepared printing papers with a variety of textures.

You can use the other drawing and painting papers as well in many cases, though the heavier ones may present problems of inking and pressing. You will want to experiment.

You can get different printing effects from unusual papers like metallic, glazed and greaseproof paper.

c   For mounting.

Use any reasonably firm paper like cartridge or sugar paper.

You can get some of the above papers from a craft shop or supplier; others from a decorator, stationer, paper-mill or printing works.

PLASTER

There are two main grades of plaster:

a   Builders' plaster. Usually pink or grey. Fairly slow setting. There are different qualities of this, with their own texture and setting properties, e.g. Sirapite, Board finish, Carlite bonding coat and finish. Your local builders' merchant will be able to advise you here.

b   Plaster of Paris, white. Fast setting and hard. There is a finer quality of this known as dental plaster.

Store plaster in a dry place.

Where plaster is mentioned in the text, use plaster of Paris or dental plaster unless stated otherwise.

You can get plaster from a builders' merchant and some craft shops or art suppliers. Chemists or drug stores sometimes stock the white plaster in small quantities, though this is a relatively expensive way of buying it if you want a lot. It is cheaper to buy it by the 1 cwt. or $\frac{1}{2}$ cwt.

c   Cellulose filler (U.K.: Polyfilla) is a specially prepared plaster. It holds very well to various surfaces and dries more slowly, which is at times an advantage. You can get it from a decorator or a craft shop.

PRINTING INKS

There are two main kinds of printing ink:
Water-based printing ink. Clean your equipment with water.
Oil-based printing ink. Clean your equipment with turps substitute or paraffin.

You can use either kind in any of the ink-printing processes mentioned, unless otherwise stated. Each can give delicate or rich effects depending on how you use it.

You can get ink in tubes or tin cans from a craft shop or art supplier.

A substitute for these is a home-made ink: mix powder paint and white paste into a thick paste. You can also use emulsion or house paint for many kinds of printmaking.

SCREWS, NAILS, PANEL PINS or FINISHING NAILS, TACKS

These all come in several sizes, of course. Use the best size for each job.

As a guide, you might like to make a collection you can add to as you need:

$\frac{1}{2}$″, 1″ and 2″ screws. These come in different gauges as well, shown by number. Numbers 6 and 8 may prove most useful.

1″ and 2″ round nails.

1″ and 2″ oval nails. These can be driven into wood without the heads showing so much.

$\frac{1}{2}$″ and 1″ panel pins or finishing nails.

$\frac{1}{2}$″ tacks.

TOOLS

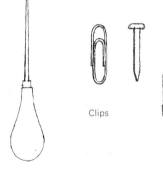

Clips

Awl (bodkin)

Awl, or bodkin. A spike for piercing, e.g. for starting off a screw in wood.
Chisel.
Clips, e.g. bulldog, foldback.
Craft knife. Where a craft knife is mentioned, use any of the following, or a similar one you have found useful: X-acto knife, Stanley knife, Swann-Morton knife, Leipzig knife. Several knives much the same are made under different names. You will find some more suitable than others for any particular job; but by and large, most will serve. For some work you can use a pen

Craft knives

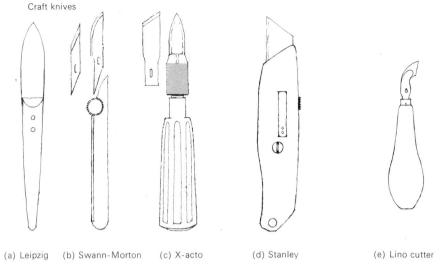

(a) Leipzig   (b) Swann-Morton   (c) X-acto   (d) Stanley   (e) Lino cutter

knife, a sheath knife, or even a No. 5 linoleum cutter in its handle.

Drill. Where a drill is mentioned, use a hand drill or a power drill, whichever you find easier or more suitable, with a drill bit for either metal, masonry or wood. These are usually in sizes up to $\frac{1}{4}''$, though there are wood bits up to $\frac{1}{2}''$. For drilling wood above this, use a brace and bit.

Glass cutter, wheel or diamond.

Hammer. There are different kinds of hammer for different jobs: Warrington hammer, for general purposes; claw hammer, for general purposes and for drawing nails or easing apart; pein hammer, for light work, especially with panel pins or finishing nails. Ash handles are best, or drop forged steel. Get the weight of hammer you can comfortably use.

Mallet. For work with chisels.

Mosaic cutter. For cutting glass and other mosaic materials.

Plaster rasp. For reducing plaster and similar surfaces.

Pliers. Many uses with metal, wire, nails, etc.

Punch. For sinking nail heads, work with metal, etc. A large nail will often serve as a punch (flatten its tip a little).

Riffler. For 'filing', in small shapes of stone, wood, etc.

Saw. Where a wood or board saw is needed, use a hand saw (or U.K. tenon saw). Where another kind is needed for a special job or with different materials, it is mentioned by name, e.g. fret saw, hacksaw. Wood saws *do* want setting and sharpening from time to time; other saws may need new blades. It makes work so much easier and quicker.

Scissors, pointed and rounded ends.

Screwdriver (A ratchet screwdriver can be used without removing the hand.)

Secateurs (or garden clippers). For cutting small branches, cane, etc.

Side cutters. For cutting wire, cane, etc.

Soldering iron. For joining wire and light metals.

Stapler. For stapling paper or card together.

Staple gun. For stapling through into board, soft wood, etc.

Stone rasp. For reducing stone and similar surfaces.

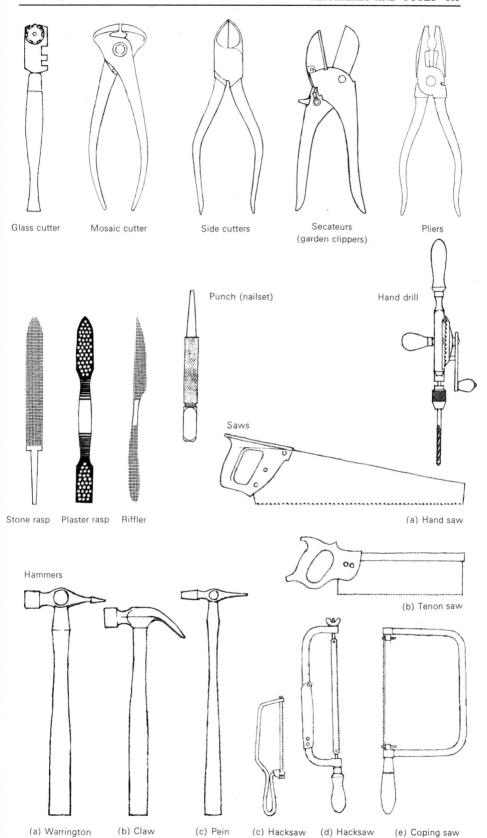

Glass cutter   Mosaic cutter   Side cutters   Secateurs (garden clippers)   Pliers

Punch (nailset)   Hand drill

Saws

Stone rasp   Plaster rasp   Riffler   (a) Hand saw

Hammers

(b) Tenon saw

(a) Warrington   (b) Claw   (c) Pein   (c) Hacksaw   (d) Hacksaw   (e) Coping saw

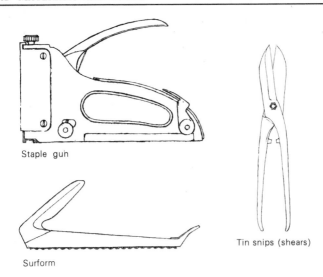

Staple gun

Surform

Tin snips (shears)

Surform or plane. For planing, smoothing wood.
Tin snips or shears. For cutting thin metal sheet.

WIRE
There are different thicknesses (or gauges) of wire, indicated by numbers (the lower the number, the thicker the wire). Use the best gauge for the job.

There are also different kinds of wire.
Brass wire.
Copper wire.
Florists' wire. In short lengths. A very fine wire.
Galvanised wire.
Soft iron wire. In short lengths. It bends easily and at angles.
Tinned wire.

You will probably find galvanised wire best for general purposes and most modelling jobs, though the others have their own special qualities. There is also a stranded galvanised wire (as used for washing lines) which can be useful at times.

If you are soldering, use a suitable wire, tinned or copper.

WOOD BATTENS, LATHS or WOOD STRIPS
Battens (lengths of wood strip) are often used in the various activities. You can get them in different widths, and you will need to choose the best one for each piece of work. Battens 1″ × ½″ are useful ones to have.

Pine or deal battens are quite suitable, unless you want a harder wood that is unlikely to split or warp, like beech or ramin. Your local Do-it-yourself shop, timber merchant or lumber yard will advise you.

Note. If you are using panel pins or finishing nails to fix a batten, slightly blunt the tips with a hammer, and don't drive them in too close to the edge of the wood. These precautions will lessen any chance of splitting.

MAIN PROCESSES

CLAY

1 Preparing a clay slab for making impressions

Have your clay in good condition (see Clay, p. 36). It is a good idea to mix some coarse grog with it if you are going to make it into a flat shape, as this helps prevent it warping; but this is not essential.

Clay
Grog

You can, if you wish, just flatten a ball of wedged clay between your hands, or press it out on a piece of hessian, hemp cloth or burlap (this stops it sticking to the table), trimming it to the shape you want afterwards with a knife.

Hessian or burlap, (hemp cloth, sacking)
Kitchen knife (craft knife)

Or you can roll it out with a rolling pin (or something that will do instead): Lay a piece of hessian or sacking flat on the table. Flatten a ball of wedged clay on the cloth and roll it once. Turn the clay over by lifting the cloth and supporting the clay with the other hand, and roll again. Continue doing this until the clay is flat. (If you want it quite level, lay two battens, the height you want it, one each side of the hessian for the rolling pin to go along, and roll out as above.)

Rolling pin (straight-sided bottle, jam jar, sawn-off broom handle)

2 battens

When the slab is flat, trim it to the shape you need with a knife. You may decide you prefer the cloth-textured side to the smooth one for making the impressions on. When you have made the impressions, let the clay slab dry out slowly and evenly from both sides.

Rolling out clay

2 Firing and decorating clay work

Let the clay work dry out thoroughly first. It is best to do this slowly by leaving it in a cool (and slightly damp) place to start with, and then bringing it out into ordinary room temperature where the air circulates—not in direct heat at all. This prevents too rapid drying and possible cracking that may follow.

a Kiln firing.

You can now biscuit fire your clay, i.e. fire it to a temperature that makes it strong and suitable for glazing. Most clays have their own best firing temperature which you can find out from the suppliers' catalogue generally. It varies a lot, though most of it fires around 1050° Centigrade (cone 03A). In this condition it is still porous and would not hold water.

Kiln
Pyrometer, temperature cones

You can load a kiln for biscuit firing without worrying about the pieces touching. You can stack them, if they are a suitable shape for stacking, and also put them inside each other; but remember that the clay will shrink: be careful not to trap one within the other, or let heavy ones stand on light ones.

Fire slowly—two or three hours at low temperature, the same at medium, and then raise to full. This is only a guide, and you should time your own firings carefully and record them as a safer guide to the performance of your particular kiln. Let the kiln cool right down before opening it and removing the ware.

You can now glaze the biscuit. This seals it and makes it vitreous.

You can get a clear glaze already made up, or mix your own from various ingredients (see book list). Soak it in water and sieve it through a 120 mesh. It should be like the top of milk so that it will lay with a good deposit on the biscuit. Then either: dip the biscuit in and out of a bowl of glaze; or put the biscuit on battens (wood strips) across the bowl and pour the glaze over it. If it is a pot, do the inside first by pouring glaze into and out of it quickly, and then do the outside. If the piece is quite small, you can apply the glaze with a flat soft brush. *Clear glaze*

120 sieve

2 bowls
Battens (wood strips)
Jug

Brush

All glazes have their best firing temperature which you can find out from the suppliers' catalogue or from your own test experiments. They vary a lot, though most earthenware glazes are between 1050°C. and 1080°C. Stoneware glazes fire above this.

When you pack a kiln for glaze firing, wipe the base of each piece quite clean of glaze deposit. Cover the kiln shelf with placing sand. Stand each piece (on stilts if needed) clear of its neighbours: no pieces must touch at any point or they will stick to each other. The glaze on them should be quite dry. *Sponge*

Placing sand
Stilts

Fire for about an hour at a low temperature to evaporate any remaining moisture and then raise to full and fire to the right maturing temperature. Turn off and let the kiln cool right down before opening the door and removing the pieces. They will still be hot!

Keep a detailed record of your glaze mixtures and the firing temperatures for future use.

To colour a glaze:

A clear glaze can be coloured with oxides before applying it. (The colour of your clay will affect the result of this—a light clay giving brighter colours.) Weigh your dry glaze powder and oxides separately (see below) and mix them together thoroughly; then carry on as above.

You can make a white or matt glaze by adding 5% tin oxide or 20% china clay (by dry weight) to the glaze powder. Some opaque glazes prepared by manufacturers are very attractive, e.g. vellum glaze. *Oxides*
China clay

To make other colours, add oxides (by dry weight):

For blue—up to 1% cobalt oxide.

For green—up to 4% copper carbonate.

For black—2% cobalt oxide, 2% iron oxide, 5% manganese oxide.

For yellow to brown—up to 5% iron oxide.

For purplish-brown—up to 8% manganese oxide.

Too much oxide will just give a metallic black. You

may like this effect; but do it with care.

Other ways of introducing colour into the clay work at different stages:

(i) Paint oxides on the green clay and biscuit fire it. Fire it again with a clear or coloured glaze if wished.

(ii) Rub oxides into impressions in the green clay and biscuit fire it. Fire it again with a clear or coloured glaze if wished.

(iii) Biscuit fire the clay. Then paint oxides on it, or rub oxides into it. Fire it again (with a clear or coloured glaze if wished).

(iv) Biscuit fire the clay. Apply clear, opaque or coloured glaze and paint into it with oxides. Then glaze fire it.

As above, keep detailed records of all your experiments.

b Sawdust firing.

Among a number of simpler means of firing is the saw-dust kiln. This is easy, cheap, exciting to do outdoors, and can be quite a social event. The clay pieces are fired by being 'cooked' in slowly smouldering sawdust. They are only soft-fired though, and are still rather brittle, but they are harder than in the green state. They come out black or grey, and can be given a nice 'polish' by burnishing afterwards with a hard smooth object like a spoon handle, or by waxing.

On a dry patch of ground out of the direct wind if possible, build a 'chimney' of bricks, leaving a small space between them for the air to get at the fire. Cover the bottom with sawdust (this should not have shavings in it) and lay some of your heavier pieces in it. Add more sawdust, packing it round and inside the pieces, so that each is in its own small world of sawdust. Continue in this way, leaving your lightest pieces to the end (they will settle during the firing and will weigh on the ones underneath). Cover finally with a last layer of sawdust.

Bricks

Sawdust

Lay kindling material (paper, dry leaves, twigs) on top and set fire to it. When it has burned away and the saw-dust caught, put a dustbin lid over the top of the chim-ney and leave the sawdust to burn through. If smoke stops coming out of the spaces between the bricks, the fire has probably gone out. Re-kindle and light it again. If the wind changes during firing, shelter it on that side or the sawdust will burn down too fast there and leave the pots 'uncooked'.

Paper, dry leaves, twigs

Dustbin (garbage can) lid

When the last of the sawdust has disappeared (it can take a full day), remove the pieces with care.

COLLAGE

1 A collage is made by sticking different kinds of material, e.g. paper, fabric, leaves, to a flat surface, using their particular qualities of shape, colour and texture to make a design.

Keep collage work as flat as possible while it is drying.

a Prepare your pieces of material by tearing or cutting, as needed.
Arrange them as you want them on the table. They can be spaced out, touching or overlapping.
Cut the right shape of paper, cardboard, board or wood to mount them on. Consider which of these is best, and what colour, in view of the collage materials you are using.
Paint or texture the mount if needed.

Transfer the arranged pieces to it and stick them into place with paste, gum or glue, whichever is appropriate. See note on these, p. 149.

Craft knife (scissors)

Paper (cardboard, board, wood)
(Saw)

Paint, texturing material with adhesive
Adhesive, spreader

b Cut a shape of paper, cardboard or board.
Without preparing a design, stick your pieces of material down with paste, gum or glue, whichever is appropriate, letting their shapes, colours and textures as you add them suggest how the design should develop.

Tools and materials as above

Think how you may want to mount or hang the collage for display, other than by pinning or stapling, and if necessary provide suitable means for this at the best stage.
A useful way to hang a light board panel for collage or other work where the surface is to be covered with materials is to make two small slots in the board before you start and pass a loop of tape through each, folding the two ends back and glueing them at the front, leaving just enough of a loop behind to pass the hanging thread through. (The turned ends of the tape can be reinforced by glueing a square of fabric over them if needed.)
Other means of hanging, using nylon thread, wire, screw-eyes, fixing plates, etc. will depend on the kind of panel you are using, and whether you are framing it or not.

Tape, scissors, chisel, mallet, adhesive, spreader, fabric

Nylon thread, wire, screw-eyes, fixing plates etc.

2 You can use sand, glitter, sawdust and other similar materials to make a collage or relief. They can be used in any combination to create a design.

Sand, stone dust, slate dust, brick dust, building block dust, coal dust, coke dust, clinker dust, bird-cage grit, glitter, metal filings, rust dust, sawdust, chalk dust

Cut a panel of cardboard, board or wood.
Draw a design on it, marking the areas you will want to texture with the material. Or work directly without a pre-drawn design.
Glue one area first (Scotch glue is useful here), and cover it liberally with the material.
Glue another area, and carry on in the same way until you have covered all the areas you want to.
When the material has stuck firmly, shake off the surplus. Go over again any parts that may have escaped or come out too thinly.
Colour may come into this at any stage as you see it developing, and you can paint areas before, during or after the texturing. You can paint the texture materials themselves, if needed, when they are quite dry.

Cardboard (board, wood)
Craft knife (saw)
Drawing medium
Adhesive, spreader

Paint

MOSAICS AND RELIEFS

1 A simple mosaic

This is made by fixing lots of small squarish pieces of material (tesserae) close together to a firm surface to make a design. The squares can be touching or spaced a little apart. It is often a good idea to sort out your pieces into colours and textures before you start.

Mosaic materials:
Paper, cardboard, board, linoleum, hard plastic, formica, thin metal, china, tile, glass (*care here!*), fabric, flat stone, wood, bark, shell, seed
Appropriate tool to shape the material: craft knife, scissors, saw, shears, tin snips, pliers, mosaic cutter, glass cutter, hammer

Cut the right shape of cardboard, board or wood to mount them on. Consider which of these is best, and what colour, in view of the mosaic materials you are using. It should be fairly rigid, or it may bend and loosen the pieces afterwards (you can strengthen hardboard or masonite by nailing it to wood battens first).

Cardboard (board, wood)
Craft knife (saw)

Paint the panel if needed.
Draw your design in its broad shapes on the panel. Or work directly without a pre-drawn design.
Arrange and fix the pieces with paste, gum or glue (U.S.: rubber cement) whichever is appropriate.

Battens or wood strips, panel pins or finishing nails, hammer
Paint
Drawing medium

Adhesive, spreader

2 A simple relief

This is made by fixing materials of various kinds and shapes to a firm surface to make a design. They can be spaced out, touching or overlapping.

Relief materials: any material that can be fixed to project slightly from a firm, flat surface
Appropriate tool to shape the material; see above

Cut the right shape of cardboard, board or wood to mount them on. Consider which of these is best, and what colour, in view of the relief materials you are using. It should be fairly rigid, or it may bend and loosen the pieces afterwards (you can strengthen hardboard or masonite by nailing it to wood battens first).
Paint or texture the panel if needed.
Arrange and fix the pieces to it with either an adhesive, nails, screws, staples, wire, thread or solder, depending on the materials you are using. Give this some thought before you start: you may have to prepare for the fixing at quite an early stage of the assembly. If you are using screws, wire or thread, you may need to pierce or drill the materials (and the panel) first.
You may find you want to add colour or texture to certain background areas as you go along.

Cardboard (board, wood)
Craft knife (saw)

Battens, panel pins or finishing nails, hammer
Paint, texturing material with adhesive
Adhesive, spreader or
Nails, panel pins, hammer or
Screws, awl, screwdriver (drill) or
Staples, hammer (staple gun) or
Wire, pliers, side cutters, awl (drill) or
Thread, needle, awl (drill) or
Solder, soldering iron (cold solder)

In the case of either a mosaic or a relief panel, think how you may want to mount or hang it for display, and provide suitable means for this at the best stage. See Collage, p. 166.

Materials for mounting or hanging

3 Making a plaster bed mosaic or relief

Keep your mosaic or relief fairly small at first, as bigger ones get considerably heavier. Mounting or hanging is then a problem, and will often call for efficient reinforcing. Up to 1′ longest measurement should be manageable for most materials.

Think how you may want to mount or hang the finished panel and provide suitable means for this at the best stage. A few suggestions are given in the following processes, and under Collage, p. 166, but work out the best way for your particular job.

There are different ways of making a plaster bed mosaic or relief:

a You can cast a block of plaster in a temporary mould that is removed afterwards.

Arrange your mosaic or relief pieces into a design on the table.

Cut a shape of board the same size.

Lay the board on some scrap paper.

Cut a strip of cardboard 1″ or so high, depending on how deep you want the plaster, and set it up as a wall round the board. Fix the ends with a staple or paper clip. The board should fit snugly inside it. Stop up any gaps round the bottom edges with clay or plasticine.

Mix delayed setting plaster (p. 173). Pour it into the mould to just below the top of the wall. Transfer the mosaic or relief pieces to it, sinking them slightly.

When the plaster is quite set, remove the cardboard wall. Colour the plaster (p. 173) if needed, wiping the colour off the pieces.

This cast block is all right as long as it is not knocked or dropped. You can give it more internal support by sinking a piece of chicken wire halfway into the plaster during the pouring.

If the block is to hang when it is finished, pass a loop of wire through the top of the chicken wire before you sink it in the plaster.

Mosaic or relief pieces, tools
Board, saw, scrap paper, cardboard, craft knife (scissors), stapler (paper clip)

Clay (plasticine)

Sponge (cloth)

Chicken wire, side cutters (pliers)

Wire

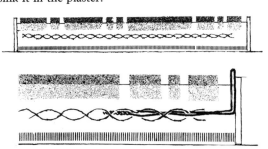

b You can cast a block of plaster in a permanent mould:
(i) Use a lid or a shallow container made of any fairly rigid material that will not soften when it is damped.

Flat tobacco tin (flat candy or biscuit tin, flat plastic or polythene food container)

Pierce two small holes in it, one either side of the centre.

Awl (hammer), wire, pliers (side cutters)

Pass a loop of wire through them and twist the ends together on the inside. This will help hold the plaster in and serve as a means of hanging it later if needed. The holes can be plugged with plasticine during the pouring stage, though they will probably be too small to let any plaster through.

Plasticine

Mark out the inside shape of the container on a sheet of paper. Arrange the mosaic or relief pieces into a design to fit it.

Pencil, paper
Mosaic or relief pieces, tools

Mix and pour delayed setting plaster (p. 173) into the mould to just below the edge. Transfer the pieces to it. Colour the plaster (p. 173) if needed, wiping the colour off the pieces.

Sponge (cloth)

(ii) Use an old picture frame with a simple right-angled moulding.

Old picture frame

Lay it face down.
Cut a piece of board to fit it loosely (hardboard or masonite is good here).

Board or masonite, saw

Cut a piece of chicken wire 1″ bigger all round than the board. Fold it round the board, bending the edges under to lie as flat as possible. Lay the board in the frame with the wired side downwards, and secure it with panel pins or finishing nails into the moulding.

Chicken wire, side cutters (pliers)

Panel pins or finishing nails, hammer

Turn the frame the right way up. Pull the chicken wire a little to raise it from the board so that it will grip the plaster better when it is poured in later. Mark out the inside shape of the frame on a sheet of paper. Arrange the mosaic or relief pieces into a design to fit it.

Pencil, paper
Mosaic or relief pieces, tools

Mix and pour delayed setting plaster (p. 173) into this 'frame mould' to just below the edge. Transfer the pieces to it.

When set, colour the plaster (p. 173) if needed, wiping the colour off the pieces.

Sponge (cloth)

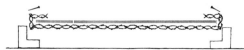

(iii) Arrange the mosaic or relief pieces into a design. Cut a corresponding shaped panel of chipboard, block-board or wood.

Mosaic or relief pieces, tools
Chipboard (blockboard, wood), saw, battens, nails (panel pins), hammer

Cut two thin battens or wood strips and nail them parallel across the panel, dividing it into three.
Cut a piece of chicken wire 1″ or so bigger all round than the panel. Lay it over the battened side, and bend the edges under the back. Staple them to the panel.

Chicken wire, side cutters (pliers), staples

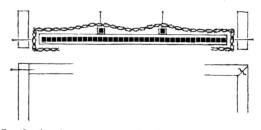

Cut further battens or wood strips to go round the sides of the panel. They should be a little deeper than you want the plaster to be. Mitre or butt join them at the

Wood chisel, mallet

corners. Fix them to the sides of the panel with counter-sunk screws or oval nails. Fill in any holes with cellulose filler or Brummer stopping, and sandpaper them flush when dry.

Screws, awl, screwdriver, countersink drill
or
Oval nails, cellulose filler (Brummer stopping), sandpaper

Mix and pour delayed setting plaster (p. 173) into the frame mould. Transfer the pieces to it.
Colour the plaster (p. 173) if needed, wiping the colour off the pieces.

Sponge (cloth)

c Make a plaster skimmed panel–for light materials only.
Arrange the mosaic or relief pieces into a design.
Cut a corresponding shaped panel of board or wood.

Mosaic or relief pieces, tools
Board (wood), saw

Sandpaper the edges.
Cut a piece of muslin or cheese cloth or scrim large enough to cover the panel and turn over the edges.
Glue the panel (Scotch glue is useful here), using a broad brush. Lay the muslin into it, working it flat and sticking the turned over edges as well.

Sandpaper

Muslin, cheesecloth (scrim), scissors
Glue, broad brush

(Nail any hardboard or masonite or thin wood panel down to battens or lath strips to prevent warping. You can also safeguard against warping later by painting the back of the panel with the same coats as the front).

Battens or lath strips, nails (panel pins), hammer

Mix delayed setting plaster or cellulose filler and add emulsion paint in roughly equal parts. Brush the mix-ture generously and evenly over the panel. It will re-main soft for an hour or so. Transfer and press the mosaic or relief pieces into it.

Plaster and size (cellulose filler), emulsion paint

You can fill in between the pieces with plaster or cellu-lose filler, raising its level more, though it is best to fix retaining battens or wood strips round the panel first if you are going to do this–or have it in a simple frame–to prevent crumbling at the edges.

Battens, wood strips (frame) nails (panel pins), hammer

4 Making a mosaic by the reversing process

NB Again be careful about the size. Keep work to a small scale to start with.
Cut two shapes of board (hardboard or masonite are best) the size you want your mosaic.

Board, saw

Arrange the mosaic pieces into a design on one of them.
The pieces could be about $\frac{1}{4}"-\frac{1}{2}"$ deep.

Mosaic pieces, tools

Glue a sheet of brown paper and stick it well down onto the mosaic, being careful not to disturb the pieces.
When it has dried, lay the other piece of board on top and turn the 'sandwich' over. Remove the board that is now on top. The underside of the mosaic is facing upwards.

Brown paper, scissors, Scotch glue, brush

At this stage, you are ready to back the mosaic with a binding material, depending on its size and weight, and where you want to use it.
(i)   Plaster of Paris.
(ii) Ciment fondu (U.S.: cement mix).
(iii) Fibre glass (included here as it is possible to make a transparent screen with it if you are using glass for the mosaic pieces and want to erect it against the light. It is, in any case, a strong, light-weight material for backing).

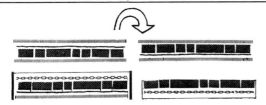

(i) For plaster of Paris:
Cut a cardboard strip 1″ or so wide and fix it as a wall round the mosaic. Fasten it with staples or a paper clip. Stop up any gaps round the bottom edges with clay or plasticine.

Cardboard, craft knife (scissors), stapler (paper clip) Clay (plasticine)

Cut a shape of chicken wire that will just fit inside the wall. This will reinforce the plaster.

Chicken wire, side cutters (pliers)

Mix plaster of Paris or dental plaster (p. 172).
Pour it into the 'mould'. When it is halfway up the wall, lay the chicken wire into it and continue pouring. Level off the top surface by patting with the flat of the hand. When the plaster has set, turn it over; remove the brown paper by soaking it first with a wet sponge, and fill in (grout) between any of the pieces that may still need it with more of the mix.

Sponge

Colour the plaster (p. 173) if needed, wiping the colour off the pieces.

(ii) For ciment fondu:
You can buy ciment fondu (or cement mix) from a builders' merchant in 1 cwt. or smaller bags. It sets off in a few hours, and then gets hard very fast.

Ciment fondu or cement mix, sand

The sand you use with it should be clean and dry.
Add 1 part of ciment fondu or cement mix to 3 parts of sand. Mix them up well, then stir in a little water — just enough to make the mix workable: not too stiff, not too sloppy. You can mix small quantities by hand in a bowl, larger quantities with a shovel or spade on a board.

Bowl (board, shovel or spade)

Then do the same as for plaster (above).

(iii) For fibre glass:
Protect your hands and wrists by rubbing a barrier cream into them.

Barrier cream

Cut three sheets of chopped strand mat the same size as the mosaic.

Chopped strand mat, scissors

Mix laminating resin and hardener (1 ounce of resin to 6 drops of hardener). There are useful calibrated paper cups for measuring out the resin. The working life of this mixture is about half an hour, so it must be used fairly quickly.

Laminating resin, hardener Calibrated paper cup

Coat the back of the mosaic with the mix and lay the first chopped strand mat in it. Work it well in. Apply more resin mix and lay in the second and third layers of mat in the same way. Trim off any ragged edges with scissors.

Brush

When it has set, turn it over and remove the brown paper by soaking it with a wet sponge or cloth. Fill in between the mosaic pieces with cellulose filler and a suitably coloured emulsion paint.

Sponge (cloth) Cellulose filler, emulsion paint

Clean off finally with a damp sponge.
Clean tools with polyester resin solvent.
If you are using glass mosaic pieces, this can now be erected as a transparent screen. (You should plan how you will do this from the start, and make provision for containing or mounting it at an early stage.)

Materials and tools for mounting

PAPIER MACHE

1 In layers

Mix some paste (p. 149).
Tear newspaper into pieces or strips a few inches across and lay them in a flat bowl of paste to be soaking. Lay them onto the surface you are covering, overlapping them slightly, and press them well down. Cover the whole surface once.

Paste, bowl, newspaper

Repeat with a second layer, covering the whole surface again. This second layer could be of kitchen paper, paper towelling or white or coloured newsprint: the change of paper shows up any parts you may have missed.

Paper towelling, kitchen paper (white or coloured newsprint)

Continue pasting (with alternate layers as above if preferred) until there are five or six layers altogether—more perhaps for a big shape. Make sure each layer is well stuck down.

You may like to finish off with a smoother layer of tissue paper. This can also give an overall colour to your model.
Paint or texture the finished model if needed.

Tissue paper

Paint, texturing material with adhesive

2 Pulped

Tear newspaper into small pieces.
Soak them in a bucket of water for a day or so—or boil them in a pan for an hour or so.

Newspaper
2 buckets
Pan

Shred and pulp the paper thoroughly by working it with the hands. Squeeze out excess water, and put the pulp in another bucket.

Mix some paste (p. 149) in the first bucket and add it to the pulp, working it all well together. It should not be too stiff or too sloppy.

Paste

Use it the same day, or keep it covered with a plastic sheet.
You can mix plaster (builders' quality will do) and add it to the pulp to make it 'model' better.

Polythene or other plastic sheeting
Plaster, bowl

PLASTER

Mixing

If you are mixing plaster to use freely in any of the modelling processes, judge how much you could safely use before it hardens and becomes useless (this won't be much, probably). Measure and pour out a little less than this of water into a mixing bowl.

If you are mixing plaster for a mould in any of the casting or mosaic processes, measure and pour out into a mixing bowl a little less water than you think it would

Mixing bowl

take to fill the mould. As a guide, 5 fluid ounces of water makes plaster to fill a mould $4'' \times 3'' \times 1''$. In practical terms this would represent a small yoghourt container, or tea-cup to a flat 2 ounce tobacco tin. Though you will generally want more than this, of course.

Measure

Have your plaster in a container beside your mixing bowl.

Sprinkle plaster onto the water, distributing it evenly.

Plaster, damp-proof container

(a) Plaster container
(b) Mixing bowl
(c) Washing up bowl

Do not stir it at all yet, or touch the water with your hands. Continue adding plaster until it has risen level with the surface of the water. **Now** stir by hand, agitating the plaster from below the surface to avoid creating air bubbles. Dissolve any lumps that may have formed, though there should not be many if you have added the plaster evenly.

The plaster is now ready to use, and you should use it at once as it is already beginning to harden.

If you need to mix and apply more plaster, leave the first layer rough to help 'key' the next. Clean the mixing bowl thoroughly in a separate washing up bowl; dry the hands; mix up the extra plaster and use it.

Wash the mixing bowl finally (and anything else you have been using) in the washing up bowl. Let the bits settle. Drain off the water and throw away the sediment in a container, NOT in the sink.

Washing up bowl

Note. Steel wool in the sink outlet will prevent any plaster that *does* get in there from clogging it. If sink has a sediment trap this will prevent problems.

Steel wool

Delaying the setting time

You will sometimes need to delay the setting time of white plaster in order to finish the work you are doing with it. (Builders' plasters are slower setting either way.)

Heat a little Scotch glue or size.

Mix your plaster as above, and add a spoonful of the glue or size. A tablespoonful in a pint of plaster-mix will delay its setting for about an hour.

Scotch glue (size, pan), Spoon

Stir from time to time with the spoon.

Colouring plaster

Use ink, dye, water colour or thinned powder paint or emulsion paint for most jobs.

Ink (dye, water colour, powder paint, emulsion paint)

You can apply the colour by dipping (if the object is small), pouring, sponging or brushing on, whichever seems appropriate. Work boldly, or the colour goes patchy.

Bowls, sponge (brush)

The effect of putting colour on dry plaster will be different from putting it on plaster that has not dried out completely, or that you have soaked after it has dried out.

Making a plaster cast of clay impressions, etc.

Cut a strip of cardboard 1″ deeper than the clay slab. Score and bend the strip to go round the clay as a retaining wall. Fasten the ends with a stapler or a paper clip. Press small wads of clay round it outside to seal and keep it snugly in place.

Cardboard
Craft knife (scissors)
Stapler (paper clip)
Clay

Mix the plaster (p. 172).

Pour it onto the clay at one point, letting it flood naturally over the surface until it is almost up to the top of the wall. Pat it in the middle with the flat of the hand to make it go into all corners. Don't dabble in it though; the top surface should find its own level.

When the plaster has set, peel off the wall, turn the block over and clear the clay away, using a stiff brush under the water tap to get into small places.

Stiff brush

Colouring or decorating a flat plaster cast

The plaster can be damp or dry for this, unless specially stated. The effects will just be a little different:

a Roll water-based printing ink onto the surface with a lino roller, leaving the depressions in the block white.

Inking plate, water-based printing ink, roller

b Flood the cast with ink, dye, water colour or thinned powder paint.
When dry, wipe the flat surface clean, leaving the depressions coloured.

Ink, (dye, water colour, powder paint), flat foam sponge

c Rub dry powder paint into the depressions—best done while the plaster is still a little damp.
Wipe the flat surface clean.

Powder paint

Flat foam sponge

d Rub wax polish into the flat surface—the plaster should be dry for this.
Flood it with ink, dye, water colour or powder paint. The wax will resist the colour, and also produce a surface quality of its own.

Wax polish, cloth

Ink (dye, water colour, powder paint)

e Melt down the unusable ends of wax crayons, white or coloured candles, or paraffin wax. Do this in a tin can in a pan of water (*being careful of fire hazard*). The plaster should be dry.
Pour the melted wax into the depressions.
When it has set off, clean the surface of the block with a flat scraper, and maybe fine sandpaper afterwards.

Wax crayon ends, (candles— white or coloured, paraffin wax), tin can, pan

Scraper, e.g. a flat piece of tin, sandpaper

f Glue carefully inside the depressions and then fill them with a suitable granular material. See list under section of Collage p. 166.
When dry, tip the surplus out, leaving a texture coating inside. Only glue a few at a time.
You can colour the top surface if needed, e.g. by process **a** above.

Adhesive, spreader
Texturing materials

PRINT MAKING

1 Making a print

a Using a small object or block that you can hold
while printing:
Prepare a pad of foam plastic or felt in a shallow
container.

Soak the pad with ink, dye or powder paint.
Lay printing paper on the table.
Press your object or block into the pad and print
directly onto the paper to make a single design or a
repeated design in any chosen arrangement of the
shapes. Re-ink whenever needed.

Shallow container like a tin
lid, a piece of foam plastic
or felt, scissors
Ink (dye, powder paint),
Printing paper

b Using a small flat object or block:
Put out printing ink on a plate.

Inking plate: glazed tile,
piece of formica or hard
plastic, zinc or other metal
plate, piece of linoleum,
hardboard (masonite) or
wood—sealed with primer,
emulsion or house paint,
small furniture panel, plate
glass, ordinary glass—if it
is safe to use . . . almost
any flat, smooth impervious
surface
Newspaper, printing ink,
roller(s), printing paper

Lay your object or block on newspaper, face up. Ink a
roller and go over its surface, inking it evenly.
Lay the printing paper on a flat surface.
Turn the object or block over and press it, by hand or
with a clean roller, directly onto the paper as above.
This works all right with small blocks, but results can
be patchy with larger ones. It sometimes helps to pad
under the printing paper with a few sheets of newspaper.

c Using a larger flat object or block:
Prepare the surface to be printed from.
Lay it on newspaper, face up.
Put out printing ink on a plate.
Ink a roller and go over the surface of the block,
covering it evenly.
Lay the printing paper carefully on it, pressing it gently
down to stick. Work over the paper in all directions
with a clean roller or with a burnishing tool like a spoon
handle. Lift one end of the paper first: if the print is not
clear, lay it back and go over it again.
If the paper is thick, you can get an easier print by
damping it with a clean sponge first.
You can, of course, make prints in this way using a
hand proof press.

Newspaper
Inking plate, printing ink,
rollers, printing paper

Spoon

Proof press

d Make a masked print:
(i) Tear or cut some simple shapes from thin paper to
make a design.

Thin paper, scissors

Ink plate evenly and lay the paper shapes on it, pressing them down gently.

Lay printing paper over this plate and press out with a clean roller. The masked areas will remain in contrast to the rest of the inked print.

(ii) Tear or cut a shape from paper.

Put out printing ink on a plate, and a sheet of printing paper flat on the table.

Using the torn or cut paper shape to mask part of the printing paper, ink a roller and roll the colour down the edge. The masked part will not print. Move the edge and repeat the process until you have a design of the masked edges.

In the case of all the above work, keep finished prints separate until they are quite dry by pinning them up or pegging them to a line. Don't let any part of the wet faces meet.

Inking plates, printing ink, rollers, printing paper

Paper, scissors
Inking plate, printing ink, roller, printing paper

Pins (clothes' pins or pegs, bulldog clips, clamps, foldback clips, paper clips, slotted chips of cardboard, line)

2 Making a roll-through print

A roll-through print, as referred to here, is one you make by rolling out a print *through* the paper rather than printing *onto* the paper.

Prepare the surface you want to print from. It should have a definite relief quality, e.g. a string collage.

Lay it flat on a board.

Lay or pin a larger sheet of printing paper over it.

Put out printing ink on a plate.

Very lightly and evenly ink a roller. Take off any surplus on some scrap paper. Over-inking of the roller will mark other parts of the paper as well.

Work carefully over the printing paper with the roller until a clear impression comes through. Accidental marking of the paper, as long as it is only light, can create interesting textural effects.

Surface to print from

Board
Printing paper, thumb tacks
Inking plate, printing ink, roller, scrap paper

3 Making a print from an uneven surface

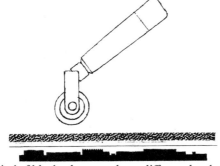

Printing from an uneven surface

This is the kind of block where you have different levels of surface, e.g. a surface built up with sand, wire and string—all different heights.

Put out printing ink on a plate.

Ink the block with a gelatine roller. You can make up a simple alternative roller for this purpose by binding a strip of foam plastic round an ordinary roller and glueing it along the edge with an adhesive.

Inking plate, printing ink
Gelatine roller (roller, foam plastic, adhesive, spreader)

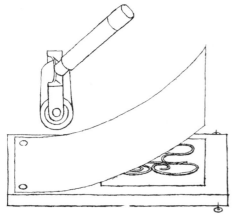

Making a roll-through print

Damp the printing paper lightly with a sponge. Lay it on the block. Lay a sheet of foam plastic over the paper and work over it evenly with an ordinary clean roller. The sheet foam plastic will force the paper down into the deeper depressions of the block.

Printing paper, sponge

Foam plastic sheet

Roller

4 Making a monoprint

Use any reasonably hard, impervious surface as a plate to print from.

Printing plate: glazed tile, piece of formica or hard plastic, zinc or other metal plate, piece of linoleum, hardboard, masonite or wood—sealed with primer, emulsion or house paint, small furniture panel, plate glass, ordinary glass—if it is safe to use

Monoprint

a Put out printing ink on another plate. Thinly ink a roller and go over the printing plate evenly. Lay a sheet of printing paper lightly on the inked surface. Hold the paper still and make a drawing on it with any slightly pointed instrument. Any *areas* that you want to darken, rub with a flattened tool or with the

Inking plate, printing ink, roller, printing paper

finger. This will give a tone effect to the line drawing. In fact, any pressure you put on the paper will pick up ink from underneath; so avoid too much accidental fingering.

Remove the paper, and the drawing will be on the underside—in reverse of course.

b You can now make a second (or negative) print from the original inked surface. **Do not ink it again.**
Lay another sheet of paper on it and go over the paper with a clean roller. The dark lines and tones that were picked up on the first print now register as light ones, giving a 'negative' effect.
This can be most attractive, and in fact you can plan to make a negative print from the start, going through stage **a** first. Experiment with different amounts of ink and different pressures with the roller.

c Put out printing ink on a plate.
Lay a printing plate on the table.
Ink a roller and go over the printing plate evenly.
Make a drawing directly into the ink with a rather blunted or flat-edged instrument, or with the finger.

Lay a sheet of printing paper on it and go over the paper with a clean roller.
Remove the paper, and the drawing will be on the underside, with some interesting 'chance' textural effects.

Matchstick (knitting needle, slip of wood or hard plastic, old ball-point pen, pencil, pencil crayon)
Flat ended tool

Printing paper, roller

Inking plate, printing plate, printing ink, rollers, printing paper

Chip of cardboard, hardboard or masonite, wood or formica, old felt tip pen

Negative monoprint

RUBBING

You can make a rubbing from some surfaces just as they are, but with others you will need to brush or clean them first to get a good impression. Use a light-weight, strong printing paper.

Brush, cloth
Good quality shelf or lining paper (detail paper, typing paper, duplicating paper)

Lay it over the surface you are making a rubbing from, and if necessary fasten it with gum-strip, sellotape (Scotch tape), drawing pins (thumb tacks) or dressmakers' pins, whichever is appropriate.
Use cobblers' heel ball (wax with black colour used by shoemakers) or a similar marking medium. Work methodically over the paper with firm, even pressure, until a clear impression comes through.
You can get a different result by using a candle to make the rubbing, and then going over it afterwards with a wash of water colour or thinned powder paint. The wax will resist the colour and remain as a contrasting design.
A rubbing can be interesting just as it is, but you may like to tear out and combine different rubbings to make a new imaginative design. Paste the pieces to a suitable mounting paper or cardboard.

Gum-strip (sellotape, thumb tacks, dressmakers' pins)
Cobblers' heel ball (wax crayon, conté crayon, terrachrome crayon)

Candle, water colour (powder paint)

Mounting paper (cardboard), adhesive, spreader

SOFT SOLDERING

Clean all meeting parts thoroughly with emery paper and a dry cloth, removing all traces of dirt, grease and rust.
Heat the tip of the soldering iron and melt some resin-cored solder on it (i.e. solder in wire form containing flux) covering the tip with a thin coating. Heat the parts to be joined with the iron, and, keeping them tightly together, use the bevelled tip of the iron to melt the solder directly onto them, so that it runs smoothly over them. (Do not put solder on the iron to take it to the join.) Keep the deposit of solder thin. Hold the join in position for a few moments until it has cooled.

Emery paper, cloth

Soldering iron, solder, pliers

SUGGESTED THEMES AND TOPICS

This is meant only as a guide to the kind of topics that might be developed with the various materials. Your own or a student's response to the material, and the feelings and ideas arising from it, are the only true guides in this respect. But it sometimes helps if the teacher can put forward a topic that his student recognises as 'right' for the material, and is happy to attempt.

Each of the following short lists of topics includes a design theme (using the material in a non-representational way), and a few topics that seem to associate in some way with the material. A number of obvious topics are omitted, e.g. An imaginary creature: these seem to invite the use of any material or combination of materials, and belong equally in any section. They are of course a source of endless inspiration among young people especially, and the reader will know of others that are as compelling.

Certain sections where a topic is self-evident (as in Study) or does not apply (as in Other Uses) are also omitted.

Asbestos
1 Arrangement of flat and corrugated surfaces
The house on the desert island
In a Druid Circle–on the mesa
A figure dressed to survive
2 Assembly of flat and corrugated surfaces
A cave dwelling
Cathedral for an unknown faith
The knight

Balloons
1 Pendent or balanced form
A space sphere
A diving sphere
A house of another time
2 Hollowed form(s)
Cave(s)
Pit(s)
Dome(s)

Bark
2, 3, 5b Arrangement of rough surfaces
Caves
The face of age
Drama underground

Beads
1, 2 Beaded surface
On a pebble beach
The bright pavilion
A journey through the planets
3 Pendent form
Rainbow rain
Swimming form
Angel

Bones
2, 3 Arrangement of articulated forms
Sea caverns
The monster and the hero
A fossil find

Bottle Caps
1, 2, 3, 5, 6 Arrangement of rounded shapes
The map of a far country
The magician's workshop
A surface to delight

Bricks
1 Form from a square block
The throne of a Viking king
Sleeping beauty
The hiding place
2 Free assembly of block forms
A building for fun
A building you can't believe
The monument

Building Blocks
1 Grey form or relief
The watcher
In the mine
Symmetry
2 Arrangement of textures
Something in the sky
Ruins
Along the shore

Buttons
1, 2, 3 Arrangement of round shapes
In stony country
The toadstool
At the control panel

Candle
1 Free flow of line
  Up a mountain
  In a stream
  Walking in space
2 A free-falling shape
  Frozen waterfalls
  A creature of the snows
  The scarecrow
3 A slim, smooth form
  The mermaid
  Submarine

Candy Sweet Wrappers
1, 2 Arrangement of (transparent) colours
  A tropical bird
  Carnival figure
  The magic castle
3 Arrangement of transparent colours
  Flames
  Seen in the sky
  The jewelled insect
4 Arrangement of transparent colours
  Cold
  Heat
  A jewel

Cane (Reed)
1 Flowing line on a surface
  At sea
  The dome
  Wheels
2 Flowing line in space
  A machine for adventurers
  A toy for the wind
  Trapeze act
  Trees in the wind

Cardboard
1, 2, 3 Arrangement of flat or rising
  planes
  Flat or rising land
  A building with unusual features
  An invented object
4 Etched colour drawing
  Windmill and wind
  The witch
  Wild plant scare!
5 Construction from planes
  A play space for animals
  Going down into a vault
  A welder at work
  Skyline

Cardboard Boxes
1, 3 Box form
  Whose house?
  Puzzle room
  Stage set
  The trap
2 Box forms
  The face of a city
  A place to spy from
  Exits and entrances

Cards (Greeting)
1 Colour and glitter
  Nearing a planet
  A visitor to a flower
  The princess
  Clown
  Ballet dancer

Cartridge Paper (Heavy Drawing Paper)
1 The facing of opposites
  House fronts – neighbours
  The mirror
  The day-and-night machine
2, 3, 4 The ice continent
  A journey of roads
  Movement patterns – waterfall,
  birdflight, traffic flow
  A ghost in daylight
5 Arrangement of spirals
  Puzzle
  Whirlpools
  Inside a clock
6 White form
  The mountain
  An invention
  A space object

Chalk
1 White form and surface
  Born in the sea
  A polar inhabitant
  The sleeper
2 White areas
  A wilderness
  The cloud giant
  A pale portrait
  Iceberg

Chicken Wire
1, 2, 3 Meshed form and surface
  Shelters
  The explorer
  The cage
  Barricade
5 Meshed areas
  A mailed figure
  A thorn hedge
  The nest

China
1 Design of sharp fragments
  An oriental palace
  The street
  The High Priest

Chippings
1 Scatter and grouping of dark fragments
  Little hill houses
  An ancient combat
  The tree

Christmas Tree Decorations
1 Scatter and grouping of shiny fragments
Daybreak
The sunshine insect
A coach for a coronation
Fairyland

Clay
1 Flow and shaping of a soft form
On the sea
Two share a secret
In the beginning of the world
2 Impressed and raised surfaces
Places to investigate
In a cupboard
A wall for pleasure
4 Arrangement of squares
Part of a town
A cargo ship
Identity parade
5 A tooled form
A hill with a path
A resting beast
A nesting bird

Coke, Coal
1, 2 Scatter and glitter of dark fragments
A house with a past
A workman
A journey to the centre of the earth

Cork, Corks
2, 3, 7a Arrangement of rough surfaces
Wild country
The home in the woods
The old gypsy
4, 5 Arrangement of smooth textures
Desert fort
A winter tree
A boat
8, 9 Arrangement of small shapes
On another planet
An object in the heavens
Vegetable stall

Corrugated Cardboard
1, 2b, 3, 5b, 6b Arrangement of parallels –
effects of light
Ploughland
Market town roofs
Building the ark
Battleground
2a Arrangement of deep spirals – effects
of light
A glimpse into the future
Lighthouse and waves
The flier in the storm cloud
Mountain ranges

Curtain Rings
1, 3 Pattern of rings
Octopus and sunken treasure
An object that ought to move
The Royal Medal

Cuttlefish Bone
1, 2 Crisp white form
The coral flower
The little boat
White Goddess
3 Surface of white scales
Inside the arctic
A ghostly apparition
The bride

Driftwood
2, 3, 4 Arrangement of eroded and
bleached surfaces
An object from the distant past
Figurehead for a ship
'It came up out of the sea'
5 The tower of gems
Totem to the sea
Hidden treasure

Egg Boxes
1, 2, 3 Platforms and wells – effects of
light
Architecture of a far-off country
A space platform
A dangerous journey

Egg Shells
1 Fragments and areas
A haunt of wild things
Desert
War
2 Domes and hollows – effects of light
Up-and-down land
Defence against attack
The invaders are colonising!

Fabric
1, 2, 4 Arrangement of colours and
textures
On the moor
Unexplored island
Fire
7 Gathering of circles
The sky and its worlds
Street lamps
8 Flow and colour of line
The dream
Creation

Feathers
2, 3, 4a Arrangement of soft textures
Portrait with a hair style
The fountain
Trees that brush clouds
Fireworks

Felt
1, 2 Arrangement of bright colour shapes
Landscape in a magic world
The Royal Person
Journey in a Great Balloon
3a Soft coloured form
City on a soft planet
An exotic vegetable
The incredible armchair

3b Soft coloured shape
   King of the Night Moths
   In a tropical fish tank
   The butterfly collection

Film
1, 2 Arrangement of glossy shapes –
   effects of light
   Windows
   Winter evening
   An astronaut exploring
3 Bright lines in the dark
   The night insect
   Devil face
   A gem

Fishbones
1, 2 Arrangement of branched lines
   The derelict boat
   A visitor from the unknown
   Tree forms
   The hedgehog
3 Movement of line through colour
   Skies
   Water
   A face in a dream

Formica
1, 2, 4 Arrangement of gay surfaces
   The wizard in his consulting room
   Fairground caravans
   The ingenious toy

Furniture
1, 3 Assembly of past constructions
   An ornate building
   Boys' Town
   A place in a nightmare
2 A form from furniture
   In the palace

Glass
1 Arrangement of reflecting and
   transparent surfaces
   Queen of Egypt
   Treasure!
   The magic mirror
   Trip to the moon
2 Arrangement of coloured light areas
   The Windows of the Weather Man

Hardboard (Masonite)
2, 3 Arrangement of hard surfaces
   A land of plains and plateaux
   Pyramids and temples
   Little home in a landslide

Jars
1, 2 Tower of coloured or textured light
   Wall of coloured or textured light

Leaves
2, 3, 5a, b, 6a Arrangement of veined
   shapes
   Stampede of all the prairie
   Flying kites
   The elf house

Linoleum
1, 2a Arrangement of plain and patterned
   shapes
   The circus parade
   A canal barge
   Roofs and chimneys
2b Arrangement of spirals and curves
   The labyrinth
   The printing works
   A device for looking through

Machine Parts
2, 3, 4, 5 Arrangement of engineered
   shapes
   The mechanic
   The battle of the monsters
   Amusement arcade

Magazines
1, 2, 5, 6 Arrangement of tone and colour
   areas
   The dream happening
3 Arrangement of spirals and curves
   Waves and whirlpools
   A bean stalk story

Matchboxes
1, 2, 3, 4, 5, 6 Arrangement and design
   from box shapes
   Homes for a hundred
   The Idol
   Fortifications

Matches
1, 2, 5b Arrangement with short lines
   Backyards and fences
   The bicycle
   A pier

Metal Scrap
2, 3, 4 Arrangement of abandoned shapes
   A neglected place
   War god
   Not in the botany book

Nails
1a Arrangement of erect lines
   Wheatfields
   A place to get lost in
   People waiting
1b Tensions between points
   A place to get trapped in
   The device to make music
   Communications
1c Design of short lines
   The timber yard
   Tribal chief
   The battle engine
2, 3a Arrangement of dots
   Tracks of journeys
   The night sky
   The firework

Newspaper
1 Arrangement of tone areas
   At the wedding
   Winter
   A group of people

2a, b Modelled form
Soft furniture
Unidentified object!
On the sea bed
2c Modelled surfaces
Creature of the rocks
Living underground

Nut Shells
1, 2 Surface of hollowed shapes
A waterless country
The forsaken castle
Portrait of an old seaman
3 A form of hollowed shapes
The gnome
The prospector
The Danger Rock

Nylon Stockings
1, 2 Arrangement of gauze areas
A home in the winds
Sea folk in a gale
The flood
3 Soft form
A figure for dressing up
The quaint arrival

Packing Straw
1 Arrangement of textures and lines
The fast stream
Flying an old aeroplane
Portrait of a farmer
2 Modelled form
The giant
The dwarf
A mysterious parcel

Perforated Zinc (meat safe sheeting)
1, 4, 5, 6 Arrangement of perforated
shapes
An armoured figure
The trappers
The dragon
3 Design of crossing and radiating lines
The sea urchin
An insect
Heraldic device

Plants
2, 3, 4 Arrangement of shapes and
patterns of growth
A scare in the skies
Dressing up
The antique piece of furniture

Plaster
1, 2 Forms and modelled surfaces
A traveller from space
The ghost ship
In the operating theatre
3 Form from a block
An opening bloom
A monument to an explorer
The cave

Plastic Dispensers
1, 2 Arrangement of curved and rounded
surfaces
A protected figure
City of towers
Irrigations

Plasticine
Animals, people, objects, places

Plastics
1, 2, 3 Arrangement of smooth surfaces
The diver
A roundabout
Tracking a satellite

(Expanded) Polystyrene (Styrofoam)
1a, 2, 4a, b, c, d Arrangement of white
or coloured surfaces
The quarry
Arctic seas
The Snow King

Potato
1 Rounded and sided form
A home for a small thing
2a An alien
An object to be careful of
b Radiating construction
A shape for exploring
An object to rock
3a, b Hollowed and raised surface
Steps to nowhere
A fun fair machine
c Hollowed form
Steps down
A star-burst
4a, b, c, d, e Arrangement of colour
shapes
A garden
The crowd
An event in the sky
f Design of rocking lines
Trails
g Design of flooded colour
Inside a flower
A natural disaster

Records
1, 2, 3 Arrangement of black shapes and
textures
The monk
Chrysalis
Skin diving for shark

Reels, cotton/spools
1 Arrangement of divided cylinders
Machinery
The devil scarer
A building with a special purpose
2 Colour column
Totem pole
The fun fair
3, 4a Pattern of circles
Boulder Beach
The machine
Holiday for spheres

Rug Canvas
1b Design of crossing and radiating lines
The amazing insect
Sea plant
The new star
2, 3 Arrangement of meshed areas
Winter trees
Shapes at night

Salt
1, 2 White form
The throne
The shell

Sand
1, 2 Arrangement of sharp textures
Volcano island
In the warren
Demolition

Sawdust
1 Arrangement of soft textures
Visit to the moors
The dead planet
Buried history
2 Soft textured form
The wild one's hide-out

Scraps
1, 2, 3 Design from familiar shapes
Fantasy land
A vehicle for fun
The conjurer

Seeds
1 Crowded areas
Houses of the ancient kingdom
The big brooch
On the bottom of the pond

Shavings
1 Arrangement of strips, curves and coils
Above the rooftops
Freight train
Adventure with a hair style

Shells
2, 3, 4, 5 Arrangement of smooth and rough surfaces
Rock plant
An antique object
Earthquake

Silver Paper, Metal Foil
1, 2, 4 Arrangement of shining areas
Tournament
The ice breaker
The cornfield

Slate
1, 2, 5 Arrangement of hard flat shapes
Land in upheaval
The battleship
Dinosaur
4 Hard grey form
Emblem of a conqueror
Home for a hermit
Effigy

Soap
1 Form of smooth surfaces
A small demon
The lamp

Spills (wood splinters)
1, 2 Arrangement of straight strips
Pylons
In a boatyard
The clown's bicycle

Stone
a Stone form
Hiding
Guardian
The rest
b Stone surface
The queue
Part of the town
The small orchestra

Stones
2, 3 Arrangement of hard forms
Flowers of Pompeii
Wrestlers
Beast from the deep

Straws
1 Movement of blown lines
Explosion
The old building
The rookery
2 Arrangement of straight and bent lines
Marriage of the scarecrows
The timber yard
The tree
3 Open framework of lines
Somewhere to live
The air machine
Design for a new star

String
1a, b, 3 Arrangement of flowing lines
Paths to everywhere
Hills
The fallen tree
1c Directions and tensions
An instrument
The archer
Long waves
6 Movement of line in space
The illuminated screen
Trapeze

Sugar (construction) Paper
1, 2 Arrangement of coloured areas
Our street
The family
Games

Thread
1, 2 Tension and curving of straight lines
Spires and domes
The lode star
A little boat off Cape Horn
3b, 4b Free movement of line
Movement of hills, skater, wild plants

Tiles
1, 2, 3 Arrangement of flat shapes
 Tree by the water
 The excavations
 A tumbledown tower

Tin Cans
1a, b, d, 3d Arrangement of reflecting
 cylinders
 The weapon
 On another planet
 Heavy industry
1c, 2, 3d Arrangement of reflecting
 surfaces
 The reservoir
 Bright flowers
 The armourer
1e, 3d Arrangement of crushed forms
 High seas
 The ogre at home
 Primeval event
3a, d Assembly of reflecting cylinders
 The observatory
 Bodyguard
 Glacier valley
3b, c, d A crushed form, assembly of
 crushed forms
 The island
 The disabled weapon
 The old secret place
4a Movement of colour
 Highways
 Rolling seas
 Flames
c Arrangement of dots
 Starfish
 The night sky

Tissue Paper
1a, b Arrangement of colour areas
 The procession
 Underground
 Music
1c Arrangement of coloured textures
 Jungle
 In the aviary
 In the volcano
2 Arrangement of transparent colours
 A night tenement
 Midnight camping site

Twigs
1, 4 Arrangement of growth lines
 The bridge
 A small crowd
 The boat

Vegetables
2, 3, 4 Rounded and sided form
 Earth god
 Earth demon
 A small creature's home
5 Arrangement of colours and textures
 The waste ground
 Different kinds of weather

Wallpaper
1, 2, 3 Arrangement of colour and
 texture areas
 Town corner
 The fighting ship
 An occasion with flags

Wax
1 Free-flowing form
 The house under the sea
 A disturbing object
 Winter visitor
2 Free-flowing line
 Spires and pinnacles
 Life in the air
 Wild plants
3 Smooth form
 A new bloom
 Designed for space

Wax Crayons
1, 2 Colour on colour
 Bonfire night
 The gay building
 Jungle

Wire
1, 3 Lines on a surface
 Cathedral front
 Suspension bridge
 The navigator
2a, b, c, d Lines in space, forms
 Bird of prey
 Lair of the unknown beast
 Derelict vehicles
e Packed form
 Deep sea diver
 Monster

Wood
a Wood form, grain and light
 A draped figure
 A moving animal
 An object to hold
b Wood surface, grain and light
 Waves and rocks
 Animals moving
 Plant riot

Wood Boxes
1 Assembly of box forms
 Living above each other
 The look-out on all sides
 Hide and seek building
2 Three-dimensional colour
 The sides of a character
 The sequences of dreaming
 Different points of view

Wood Off-cuts and scraps
1, 3 Arrangement of projecting forms
 Old town, new town
 The fisherman and his boat
 An object to look into

2 Contrasts of wood surface
Main line tunnel
An abandoned house
Storm hill
4, 5a, b, c Arrangement of textures and
lines
On the sea
In the sky
The tramp

FURTHER READING

Brass rubbing
Brass Rubbing by M. Norris, *Studio Vista*, UK/*Dover*, US

Carpentry
Boys' and Girls' Book of Carpentry by J. Taylor, *Acorn*

Collage
Collage by F. Brow, *Pitman*
Creating in Collage by N. d'Arbeloff and J. Yates, *Studio Vista*, UK/*Watson-Guptill*, US
Curve Stitching (Mathematical topics 2nd yr. Book 2) by E. James, *Oxford University Press*

Drawing and painting
Basic Design by M. de Sausmarez, *Studio Vista*, UK/*Reinhold*, US
Exploring with Paint by Petterson/Gerring, *Studio Vista*, UK/*Reinhold*, US
Creative Pencil Drawing by P. Hogarth, *Studio Vista*, UK/*Watson-Guptill*, US
Materials of the Artist by M. Doerner, *Hart Davis*, UK/*Harcourt Brace*, US
Complete book of Artists' Techniques by K. Herberts, *Thames and Hudson*, UK/*Praeger*, US
Painters' Pocket Book by H. Hiler, *Faber and Faber*, UK/*Watson-Guptill*, US
Creative Drawing–point and line by E. Röttger, *Batsford*, UK/*Reinhold*, US
Creative Crayon Craft, *Cosmic Crayon Co.*
Acrylics by J. Mills, *Pitman*

Embroidery
Teaching Children Embroidery by A. Butler, *Studio Vista*

Fabric
Fabric Printing by Hand by S. Russ, *Studio Vista*, UK/*Watson-Guptill*, US
Batik Art and Craft by Krevitsky, *Reinhold*
Colour and Texture in Creative Textile Craft by R. Hartung, *Batsford*, UK/*Reinhold*, US
Dyed and printed fabrics by J. Hobson, *Dryad*
Tie and Dye by A. Maile, *Mills and Boon*, UK/*Taplinger*, US
Fabric Pictures by E. Alexander, *Mills and Boon*, UK/*Hearthside*, US
Batik Fabrics by J. Hobson, *Dryad*
Textile printing and dyeing by N. Proud, *Batsford*, UK/*Reinhold*, US

Mosaics
Making Mosaics by J. Berry, *Studio Vista*, UK/*Watson-Guptill*, US
Pottery and Mosaics by H. Powell, *Blandford*, UK/*Branford*, US
Mosaics by R. Williamson, *Crosby Lockwood*
Mosaic Making by H. Hutton, *Batsford*, UK/*Reinhold*, US
Making Mosaics by Arvois, *Oak Tree*

Paper sculpture
Paper Folding by Murray and Ripney, *Dover*
Creative Corrugated Paper Craft by R. Hartung, *Batsford*, UK/*Reinhold*, US
Origami–Birds, Flowers, Animals and Fishes, *Methuen*
Make it in Paper by M. Grater, *Mills and Boon*, UK/*Taplinger*, US
Chinese paper cut Pictures by N. Kuo, *Tiranti*
Fun with Paper Modelling by G. Payne, *Ward*, UK/*Frederick Warne Inc.*, US
Creating with Paper by P. Johnson, *Kaye*, UK/*University of Washington Press*, US
Take an Egg Box by R. Slade, *Faber and Faber*, UK/*Lothrop, Lee and Shepherd*, US
One piece of Paper by M. Grater, *Mills and Boon*, UK/*Taplinger*, US
Creative Paper Craft by E. Röttger, *Batsford*, UK/*Reinhold*, US
Papercraft by D. Meilach, *Pitman*

Pottery
Practical Pottery and Ceramics by Kenneth Clark, *Studio Vista/Viking*
Beginning at the Beginning with Clay by S. Robertson, *S.E.A.*
Simple Pottery by K. Drake, *Studio Vista*, UK/*Watson-Guptill*, US
Clay and Terracotta by J. Newick, *Dryad*
Pottery Materials and Techniques by D. Green, *Faber and Faber*, UK/*Praeger*, US
Technique of Pottery by D. Billington, *Batsford*, UK/*Hearthside*, US
Pottery by M. Fieldhouse, *Foyle*
Understanding Pottery Glazes by D. Green, *Faber and Faber*
Potter's Book by B. Leach, *Faber and Faber*, UK/*Transatlantic*, US

Pottery in the Making by D. Lunn, *Dryad*
Clay and Glazes for the Potter by D. Rhodes, *Pitman*, UK/*Chilton*, US
Pottery without a Wheel by K. Tyler, *Dryad*
Young Potter by D. Baker, *Ward*, UK/*Frederick Warne Inc.*, US
Beginners' Book of Pottery by H. Powell, *Blandford*, UK/*Emerson*, US
Pottery and Once-Fired Method by A. White, *Dryad*

Printmaking
Simple Printmaking by Kent and Cooper, *Studio Vista*, UK/*Watson-Guptill*, US
Frontiers of Printmaking by M. Rothenstein, *Studio Vista*, UK/*Reinhold*, US
Creative Printmaking by D. Green, *Batsford*, UK/*Watson-Guptill*, US
Making Colour Prints by J. Newick, *Dryad*
Young Printmaker by H. Weiss, *Kaye*, UK/*Wm. R. Scott*, US
Lino Cuts and Wood Cuts by M. Rothenstein, *Studio Vista*, UK/*Watson-Guptill*, US
Wood cut by H. Sternberg, *Pitman*
Creative Printmaking by M. Andrews, *Prentice Hall*
Printmaking Today by J. Heller, *Pitman*
Printmaking by D. Meilach, *Pitman*

Puppetry
Chinese Puppet Theatre by Obraztsov, *Faber and Faber*, UK/*Plays Inc.*, US
Hand and String Puppets by W. Lancaster, *Dryad*
Practical Puppetry by J. Mulholland, *Jenkins*
You Can Make a String Puppet by R. Slade, *Faber and Faber*
Book of Puppetry by Bufano, *Collier Macmillan*

Sculpture
Sculpture in Wood by E. Norman, *Tiranti*
Woodcarving by A. Durst, *Studio Vista*, UK/*Viking*, US
Whittling and Woodcarving by B. Tangerman, *Dover*
Direct Carving in Stone by M. Batten, *Tiranti*
Sculpture at your Fingertips by F. Press, *Reinhold*
Sculpture for Beginners by M. and L. Divalentin, *Oak Tree*
Direct Metal Sculpture by Meilach/Seiden, *Allen and Unwin*
The Young Sculptor by H. Weiss, *Kaye*, UK/*Wm. R. Scott*, US
New Materials in Sculpture by H. Percy, *Tiranti*
Creative Clay Work by H. Isentein, *Oak Tree*
Materials and Methods in Sculpture by Rich, *Oxford University Press*
Creative Wood Craft by E. Röttger, *Batsford*, UK/*Reinhold*, US
Creative Clay Craft by E. Röttger, *Batsford*, UK/*Reinhold*, US
Sculpture in ciment fondu by Mills, *C. R. Books*
Plaster Casting for Student Sculptor by Wager, *Tiranti*
Carver's Companion by P. Morton, *Black*

Stained glass
Stained Glass Craft by Divine and Blackford, *Warne*

Straw work
Decorative Straw Work by Davis and Sandford, *Batsford*

Woodcutting, Lino cuts,
See printmaking